DOING PHILOSOPHY

755062

DOING PHILOSOPHY

A GUIDE TO THE WRITING
OF PHILOSOPHY PAPERS

Fifth Edition

Joel Feinberg

Late Regents Professor of Philosophy and Law
University of Arizona

WADSWORTH
CENGAGE Learning·

Australia • Brazil • Japan • Korea • Mexico • Singapore • Spain
United Kingdom • United States

WADSWORTH
CENGAGE Learning

Doing Philosophy:
A Guide to the Writing of
Philosophy Papers, Fifth Edition
Joel Feinberg

Editor-in-Chief: Lyn Uhl

Publisher: Clark Baxter

Senior Sponsoring Editor: Joann Kozyrev

Assistant Editor: Joshua Duncan

Editorial Assistant: Marri Straton

Market Development Manager:
Joshua I. Adams

Brand Manager: Jennifer Levanduski

Art Director: Andrei Pasternak

Print Buyer: Sandee Milewski

Production Service: PreMedia Global

Cover Designer: Riezebos Holzbaur/
Tim Heraldo

Cover image: Book Stacks in Long Room,
Trinity College Dublin © Michael St. Maur
Sheil/CORBIS

Compositor: PreMedia Global

For product information and technology assistance, contact us at
Cengage Learning Customer & Sales Support, 1-800-354-9706

For permission to use material from this text or product,
submit all requests online at **cengage.com/permissions**
Further permissions questions can be emailed to
permissionrequest@cengage.com

ISBN-13: 978-1-285-05501-5

ISBN-10: 1-285-05501-2

Wadsworth
20 Channel Center Street
Boston, MA 02210
USA

Cengage Learning is a leading provider of customized learning solutions with office locations around the globe, including Singapore, the United Kingdom, Australia, Mexico, Brazil, and Japan. Locate your local office at:
international.cengage.com/region

Cengage Learning products are represented in Canada by
Nelson Education, Ltd.

For your course and learning solutions, visit **www.cengage.com.**

Purchase any of our products at your local college store or at our preferred online store **www.cengagebrain.com**

Printed in the United States of America
1 2 3 4 5 6 7 16 15 14 13 12

Contents

Preface

This booklet is intended to help college students who are enrolled in introductory courses in philosophy and are required to write at least one philosophical paper. A book of this kind, of course, could be used by *any* student in *any* philosophy course, beginning or advanced, or even by students who are not formal students of philosophy at all, but wish to "do philosophy" anyway. But the primary group it is designed to serve are beginning students in classes using my collection, *Reason and Responsibility*, fifteenth edition, as a text. Wadsworth Publishing Company has made this guide available, free of charge, as a supplement to *Reason and Responsibility*.

I am grateful to Tammy Goldfeld and Peter Adams for suggesting that I write the booklet, and for giving me every support and encouragement. My research assistant, Linda Radzik, made numerous helpful suggestions and guarded me from tempting errors throughout. In these, as in other scholarly matters, her assistance has been invaluable.

—Joel Feinberg

Acknowledgements for the Fifth Edition

Wadsworth thanks Justin Tosi from the philosophy department at the University of Arizona for agreeing to update *Doing Philosophy* for the fifth edition. We are pleased that his careful and judicious additions and edits will help to keep Joel Feinberg's valuable writing advice relevant to today's philosophy students.

1

Methods of Proceeding

INTRODUCTORY

Philosophical perplexity can assail anyone, from a six-year-old child who wonders how she can know that she is not really dreaming, to the victim of a painful disease who wonders how the evil in the world can be reconciled with the existence of an all-good, all-powerful deity, to the computer programmer who is tempted to the view that human beings are merely complex machines. In fact, it is difficult to conceive of any person of normal sensitivity who has not reflected on genuinely philosophical problems and grappled seriously with them. For help in that inevitable project, students study philosophy. The ultimate aim of a philosophy course is not merely to help the student understand the writings of the great thinkers of the past. It is also to give opportunity to students to try their hand at those problems themselves. This process of using discussion and essay writing to dispel, as much as possible, perplexities about the human condition is often called "doing philosophy," in the odd phrase of philosophy professors. Given the difficulty of the intellectual problems, the only hope anyone has of doing philosophy well is to get practice at it.

That is why professors like to make writing assignments even to inexperienced beginning students of philosophy. The first results of such assignments, however, are likely to be disappointing to the student and teacher alike. If a student's only model of a philosopher is Plato, or Descartes, or Hume, scholars whose own views were the results of years of deep reflection, intense conversation with learned friends, and philosophical essay and letter writing, she is likely to be overwhelmed by the challenge. Still, if students are not encouraged to do philosophy themselves on the ground that they are too inexperienced to do it well, then paradoxically they will never become experienced enough to have a remote hope of doing it well. The situation invites comparison with children who are not allowed in the water until they know how to swim.

This little book is meant to help the student in a beginning philosophy course whose text is *Reason and Responsibility*. We imagine that the student has just been assigned the task of writing a philosophical essay, say of three to five pages, or a term paper of as many as ten pages. This booklet provides not only hard and fast rules of good writing, but also informal tips and guides. The scope of our subject includes not only the writing of specifically philosophical essays, but also the production of good writing generally, whatever its subject. A poorly written paper cannot be a good philosophical paper whatever its uniquely philosophical merits may be. So we shall try to

1

help the student put into practice the principles of good writing, which of course must be included among the principles of good philosophical writing.

SELECTING A TOPIC

Choose a relatively narrow question for your essay to answer. Even if your instructor has made the assigned topic rather precise and narrow, it may be helpful to make it narrower still. There may be a controversial issue separating the philosophers who have disagreed in their answers to the assigned question, an issue that is presupposed by the assigned paper topic in the sense that *it* must be solved before the assigned problem can be solved. To say that one problem presupposes another in this sense is to say that what its correct solution is depends on what the correct solution of the presupposed problem is. Then, having identified such a problem, you may have some light to cast on it, thereby taking an important step toward its solution.

If your instructor, however, has given you much greater discretion in the choice of a topic, then the best advice one can give you is to select the question that you are most interested in. That will be to arm yourself with the best kind of motivation for working out your own belief-dispositions, straightening out their hitherto unforeseen difficulties, making them clearer and more coherent with your other beliefs. This motivation will enable the study of philosophy to perform its own special services for you, to make your work meaningful, and even exciting. If you find another philosophical problem boring, then give it wide berth if you can. Perhaps further on in your studies you will discover a significance in what is now boring that will make it seem crucial and exciting.

THE IRRELEVANCE OF MOST LIBRARY RESEARCH

Your college library may contain books, journal articles, and other online resources that could help you, but in your circumstances, that is not likely. Professional philosophers usually write for one another, not for the general public, and what they write for one another is often technical and obscure to the beginner. There are textbooks in the library too, of course, but you may find that your time is better spent rereading the assigned materials than by looking here and there in the library stacks for a book that will overcome your inertia and start the words flowing from your own intellectual pump. In the end, the creative process is almost always a simple transaction between you, the philosophical problem, and your blank paper or empty computer screen. There is no simple substitute for thinking hard, on your own. One thing is for sure: you cannot solve a philosophical problem by simply "looking up the answer in the library." Even if there were a way of looking up an answer in another writer's book, it would give you no practice at *doing* philosophy yourself, and developing your philosophical reasoning skills. If "research" is defined in terms of looking things up, then there is no such thing as "philosophical research."

In some special cases, however, library materials and online research might prove useful for your writing, especially for longer assignments that have a broader focus or require more sustained argument. In addition to textbooks, many publishers produce handbooks, guides, companions, and other relatively accessible books and journals that survey a wide range of philosophical topics and figures. There are also a number of online encyclopedias, blogs, and other sites with extensive philosophical content, such as those which are listed in Chapter 12 of this book. These may all help you to understand what distinguishes the various positions on an issue, or fill in gaps in your knowledge of the relevant philosophical literature. Assignments concerning the history of philosophy call for special consideration. Some historical figures—such as Hobbes and Hume—are famously systematic in their theorizing. Owing to this, their views in one area of philosophy might be relevant to their views in another, and so your paper might benefit from your casting a wider net in your reading. In any case, your instructor will be the best judge of whether these materials would be useful for your assignment, and so you should ask before spending much time on them.

Your library also contains biographical information about some of the philosophers you have read, their marital and domestic situations, their political and religious affiliations, the place where they lived out their lives, and the years of their births and deaths. These facts can be interesting, and for some purposes even useful, but in almost every case they will be irrelevant to your task. If your aim is to do philosophy yourself, and to do it in this instance by criticizing another philosopher's work, then get on with it. Don't delay the substantive part of your paper for digressive descriptions of facts that can have no relevance as reasons for or against the philosophical conclusions you are supposed to be criticizing.

There is another danger in padding up your paper with such irrelevancies. You may not notice that you are treating the personal attributes of a philosopher as if they really were relevant as reasons for or against his views, as when we dismiss his views as mistaken because he is known to be a liberal or because he is known to be a conservative, or because he often is emotional, or even neurotic. It may be true that his circumstances give him some self-advancing reason for wanting some conclusion to be true, or that he has some shortcoming of intellect or character, but these are judgments about *him*, not about his arguments. His arguments for some philosophical conclusion might yet be valid and the conclusion itself true even though his motives are suspect and his character wicked. To infer that his position is mistaken because of some irrelevancy in his circumstances is to commit the informal fallacy called the *argumentum ad hominem* (Latin for "argument directed at the person"—see Chapter 7). If certain facts about a philosopher will be irrelevant as grounds for accepting or rejecting his conclusions, you might as well not go to the library to look them up in the first place.

A philosophical essay, therefore, is not a so-called research paper. A chemist may go to the library to discover what other chemists have learned in their observations of some phenomenon, or she may seek to make similar observations, if possible, in her own laboratory. A historian may go to the library to examine historical documents or to learn what happened at a certain time and place. Anyone may go to the library to "look up" a certain book, or to find out what books the stacks contain on a certain subject—even on philosophy. All these uses of a library are called "research" purposes. They all call for patience, ingenuity, and scholarship. In general, research is the effort to discover facts about nature or history, not to argue for the truth or falsity of philosophical positions. Philosophical truths are not "facts" to be discovered by investigation. Rather they are truths we acquire, at least in major part, by "thinking hard," making distinctions, giving proofs, and so on. One does not go to the library to discover whether God exists, or what are the limits of human knowledge, or whether human beings have free will.

RESOLVING CONTROVERSIES

If you find after a period of intense but fruitless hard thinking that you can't find any critical arguments to employ in support of a position on the assigned topic, you may be well advised (if your instructor allows this strategy) to compare two philosophers who are in clear disagreement with one another. Then you can try to decide which philosopher has the more plausible position, and why. This is a psychological technique for knocking down barriers to the forming of your own views. You need not defend a position of your own on the problem that divides the two philosophers. Rather you can take a stand on the comparative persuasiveness of two opposed arguments, a more limited and precise question.

In *Reason and Responsibility*, you will find opposed positions by different philosophers on virtually every philosophical problem discussed there. The editor's assumption is that presenting more views than one on each philosophical question covered in the book will make it somewhat easier for the students to come to terms with the problems themselves. Moreover, it is simple fairness to give every side an equal hearing, and to give the student "customer," shopping for her own philosophy, a diverse inventory of beliefs from which to choose.

APPRECIATING PHILOSOPHERS OF
AN EARLIER PERIOD

The problem of "picking sides" in controversies between other philosophers is further complicated by the fact that some of the opposed views expressed in *Reason and Responsibility* are those of different historical epochs. One might find a seventeenth-century thinker, for example, disagreeing with a philosopher from ancient Greece. The twentieth-century British philosopher Bertrand Russell warns students of the pitfalls of such a situation and gives them exactly the right advice in a passage which (unlike most passages) warrants quotation at length:

4

In studying a philosopher, the right attitude is neither reverence nor contempt but first a kind of hypothetical sympathy, until it is possible to know what it feels like to believe in his theories, and only then a revival of the critical attitude which should resemble, as far as possible, the state of mind of a person abandoning opinions which he has hitherto held. Contempt interferes with the first part of this process, and reverence with the second. Two things are to be remembered: that a [person] whose opinions and theories are worth studying may be presumed to have had some intelligence, but that no [person] is likely to have arrived at a complete and final truth on any subject whatever. When an intelligent [person] expresses a view which seems to us obviously absurd, we should not attempt to prove that it is somehow true, but we should try to understand how it ever came to *seem* true. This exercise of historical and psychological imagination at once enlarges the scope of our thinking, and helps us to realize how foolish many of our own cherished prejudices will seem to an age which has a different temper of mind.[1]

THE OUTLINE

There is no requirement that you make an outline when you are ready to begin writing. Many writers get along fine without ever making outlines. But for others, an outline helps them see the shape of the emerging forest when not blocked from view by individual trees. The outline should contain near its beginning a precise statement of the question you will attempt to answer. Following that, at some point there should appear a preliminary statement of what your answer to that question, also called your "thesis," will be. The rest of the outline should state the reasons supporting your thesis and perhaps, if room remains, your replies to criticisms that might be made by skeptical readers. There is no reason why the author should regard the outline at this point as somehow binding. The outline is no private promise made to oneself or to anyone else. In most cases, some of its arguments will prove very difficult to state clearly. Others will turn out to be logically flawed, still others will require more length to develop than you have time to arrange. Quite apart from logical argument, parts of the emerging paper may be awkwardly written and highly inelegant. For that reason, the obscure parts will have to be rewritten, and that too might lead to some deviation from a very *nonbinding* outline. You should feel free to revise your outline as you go along. In the end, it will be hard to say which came first, the paper or the outline, and in some cases the outline will be largely *ex post facto* ("after the fact"). That matters not a bit. The point of the outline is simply to help you keep your thoughts together, to remind you of your own strategy if it should fade from view.

---

[1]Russell, Bertrand. *A History of Western Philosophy* (New York: Simon and Schuster, Inc., 1945), p. 39.

The following sentences form a kind of outline of an outline, an informal self-directed battle plan.

I. Opening paragraphs
   A. The question this essay is designed to answer (or alternatively the problem it aims to solve)
   B. The question is clarified (if necessary)
   C. If it would be helpful, an explanation of why the question is important (or interesting or difficult)
II. The writer's answer to the question (or alternatively, her thesis)
III. Middle paragraphs (the bulk of the paper):

   The writer's argument for the thesis. There is no one fixed pattern for arguments.
IV. The argument may include, but it is not required to include, a restatement and if necessary a qualification, of the thesis. Also it could include, but need not, "a reply to the critics," that is a rejoinder to arguments against the writer's thesis that were actually made by some other or earlier philosopher, or which might be made by someone of skeptical disposition.
V. Closing paragraph: A brief summary of this argument as presented in III A.

This abstract of an outline is only one among numerous formal structures that a given paper's outline might follow, depending of course on the content of the paper being outlined. Very likely, a student paper accurately condensed by the outline-abstract above would be too long, thus forcing the student-author to cut. In this case, the outline would enable the student-author to see at a glance what is most dispensable, and act accordingly. The outline might also reveal to the author that she doesn't really trust or understand her own argument. That argument may no longer seem intuitively convincing when she is able to look closely at its bare bones, so improvements or corrections will have to be made. In that case the outline, which is always tentative, may reveal a connection between statements that will not hold them together in the way required by a cogent argument, and will show the various possibilities of change that would correct the situation. The outline serves as an uncluttered statement of the logical structure of the argument. One can use it as a work sheet, moving propositions around until they seem to form a coherent argument, and then reconstructing the full paragraphs in the paper itself so as to incorporate the changes first worked out on the work-sheet (that is, on the tentative outline).

PREPARATION OF THE FINAL DRAFT

It is hard to know exactly what a complete "draft" is. If you use an outline to record your strategy and to decide upon deviations from it, and you constantly revise subsections and switch paragraphs about in order to find the most natural ordering of the points you are trying to make, you may well reach the end of your essay after many revisions in its major points. In the extreme case, so many changes will have been made that you will want to rewrite the entire paper from beginning to end. That would be to write a new "draft." Sometimes it will be necessary. More often it will not.

Your motive for typing up a final draft may be more formal than substantive. You may simply want the essay that emerges from your word processor or printer to be neat and tidy, free of messy marks, uneven margins, punctuation and spelling mistakes, and typographical errors. One graduate student, though a good typist generally, had a propensity to type a "t" when he meant to type a "w." He opened a chapter of his Ph.D. thesis by typing "not" instead of his intended "now." The sentence as it appeared on paper then read: "We are not [instead of 'we are now'] ready to consider the next problem." His supervisor then wrote in the margin: "Yes, that is true, but must you be so candid about it?" In a sense, the word "now" which the student meant to type was not misspelled. That is how one spells "not"—*n o t,* if one means *not.* A spell-check on your computer will not catch the mistake because it has no way of knowing what you meant—whether you meant *now* or *not.* The best way to prevent mistakes of this sometimes damaging kind is to look at each word and each letter, one at a time, page after page. That tedious but essential task is similar to what authors must do when they check for errors (primarily printer's errors) in the page or galley proofs that come to them from the type setter. In the publishing world that work, reserved for the author, is called proof-reading. It is done most effectively when the labor is shared by two persons, one of whom (usually the author) reads aloud from her original typescript, while her assistant looks at the printed page proofs while listening to the author's voice and spots mistakes when there are discrepancies between what he sees and what he hears. He then uses a conventional set of symbols to point out the mistakes to the printer in a marginal comment.

Students, of course, do not submit their original essays to typesetters. Still, students are as prone as other people to commit so-called typographical errors, and very often the errors are best caught and corrected by a team of two persons. One partner reads aloud from one copy produced by a computer *cum* desk printer, while the author, following an identical copy, and listening for incoherences, is ready to pounce on a typographical error when it turns up. This kind of "proof-reading" then results in the final revisions, before the paper is handed in.

7

WRITING BLOCKS

Typically, the very first thing to be done in the preparation of a philosophy essay is to write a first draft of an outline, knowing full well that what you are doing at that stage is a kind of preliminary toying with the problem, first setting it up in one way, then in another, always feeling free to knock it all over and start again. Or one can experiment similarly with the various *theses* that might be the best answers to an interesting question. At a certain point, an apparent insight comes, and in great excitement you type or write it down, determined not to lose it while it is still fresh in your mind. Very often that is how the words begin to come and what is called a "writer's block" begins to erode.

Often, however, the erosion is not produced that easily. The problem in many such cases is not a result of confusion over logic or a lack of strategies for argument and proof. The problem lies elsewhere: *in finding the right words.* Even after a preliminary outline has been completed and a central argument sketched, there are times when the words still will not come. This happens on occasion even to the most talented and experienced writers. The experience can produce frustration and despair, and these emotional states can themselves strengthen the writer's block, making the problem even worse. What then is to be done?

My best advice is simply to start writing anyway. Even if you know that you are not finding the elusive "right words," use some other words, and if your sentences at first don't express your real intended meanings, come back to them later and try new ones. Most importantly, keep reminding yourself that you are not instantly and permanently committed to these particular words. You can always change them or delete them later. Acknowledge to yourself now that you are holding yourself only to very low personal standards, but remain determined to substitute your usual high standards at some point after the block has collapsed. As you start writing with greater speed and words come in a quicker flow, you will gain more confidence and that too will contribute to the recovery of your usual prowess. Soon you will be thinking about things philosophical, and not simply about finding words. Then after you have completed the "final draft" of the paper, as your last chore connected with the project, rewrite the "temporary draft" of the first few paragraphs, just as you promised yourself earlier.

2

Rules of the Game

PLAGIARISM AS A LEGAL WRONG
(VIOLATION OF ANOTHER PERSON'S PROPERTY RIGHT)

Laws protecting authors and artists from the unauthorized publication of their works are called copyright laws. These laws give authors the "exclusive right to publish their works or to determine who may so publish."[1] When a publisher or editor wishes to reprint the published work of an author he must first have the permission of the copyright holder, for which he may be charged a permission fee. Some works are said by the courts to be the property of no one owner, but rather belong to the general public. These works include court decisions, which are said to be in "the public domain," and older works whose copyright has expired. Copyright infringement, as such, is not a crime. Rather it is the occasion for a civil suit brought by the copyright holder against the infringing party for compensatory damages, or a suit seeking an injunction that will require that the infringements cease.

In the law, then, plagiarism is a violation of a property right. At best its harm consists simply of a deprivation of the exclusive control an owner normally exercises over her property. At worst it can prevent an owner from realizing a profit that is rightly hers. In other instances it can mislead the public about the true authorship of a work, and affect the reputations of innocent parties in ways they do not deserve, for example getting credit for a good work they did not create, or blame for a poor work they did not create. Some of these harms affect private interests primarily; some affect the public interest too, especially the interest in avoiding deception about matters of fact. On the whole, there is some analogy between plagiarism and theft. There is also some analogy between plagiarism and ways of violating property rights other than by simply stealing the property from its owner, for example trespassing, and other instances of violating an owner's exclusive control, by forgery of the owner's permission, false pretenses, and so on.

---

[1] Gifis, Steven H. *Law Dictionary* (Woodbury, New York: Barrons' Educational Series, Inc., 1975), p. 46.

PLAGIARISM AS A MORAL WRONG
(CHEATING AND LYING)

When a student knowingly submits the work of another, with at most minor changes, as his own, in fulfillment of a classroom assignment, that is called "plagiarism" too. But in this case, for practical reasons the law stays uninvolved. Academic plagiarism is neither the name of a crime nor of a tort. Still, it is punished within the academic context through such sanctions as suspension and a failing grade. But there is no academic procedure awarding any victim appropriate damages. This is not to say that plagiarism has no victims. It does. The instructor has been the victim of a deception, and the implicit code of respectful exchange on which classroom instruction is based has been violated. Further, submission of a plagiarized paper is an instance of taking unfair advantage of one's fellow students. Even in cases where the cheating is not detected, one wrongs one's peers, in the same way that tax cheats and rule-breakers wrong their fellow citizens. The plagiarist has, for exclusively self-interested reasons, broken the rules of fair play and granted himself an unwarranted exemption from the requirement of doing and submitting one's own work. The kind of trust that is taken for granted at a college or university confers great benefits on everyone who participates in its academic activities. Plagiarism, like other forms of cheating, takes advantage of this trust. The erosion of this trust is a very great harm. Among other things, it creates an environment of suspicion and competition, rather than openness and cooperation, that is damaging both to student–faculty relations, and to relations among students themselves.

Plagiarism is the most serious sin of a peculiarly academic kind that one can commit. It involves quite essentially elements of misrepresentation, fraud, and cheating. It is a clear example of a dishonorable act, one that offends against the highest ideals of intellectual honesty, those to which the great scholars and scientists have dedicated their careers in centuries past.

The temptation to plagiarize another's work is often understandable. Students sometimes feel ill-equipped to handle a difficult assignment, or are anxious in the face of impending deadlines and are concerned to win the approval of an instructor, or at the very least a decent grade. But the submission of plagiarized material constitutes a kind of lying: one is deliberately creating a false impression, and in so doing seeking to benefit oneself.

Often students seem to commit this dreadful offense as if by accident or mistake. They have never heard the rules governing academic writing stated and interpreted clearly, or if they have heard, they haven't remembered, or worst of all they haven't cared. For that reason, it is probably not wise or just to inflict the most severe available punishments on them for their unethical conduct. I would vote instead for a system that contained two possible penalties for the academic sin of plagiarism. If the plagiarism is attributable, in substantial degree, to ignorance or negligence, the perpetrator would be given an automatic grade of F and denied credit for taking the course. If there is a clear and compelling reason to believe that the act was fully informed and deliberate, then the perpetrator should be suspended indefinitely from the university. Of more immediate interest, most colleges have academic honesty policies that allow for these penalties and others, such as plagiarism workshops and permanent notes on transcripts.

The Internet now constitutes a tremendous resource and temptation for those who are intent on plagiarizing. There are many websites that will sell term papers for relatively modest fees, all the while disingenuously instructing their customers not to submit such work as their own. Fortunately, there are now a large number of websites devoted to detecting these sources, and instructors, increasingly, are making use of them. Students would be well-advised to consider that if they found a resource online, so can anyone else, including their instructor.

QUOTATION, ATTRIBUTION, AND ACKNOWLEDGMENT

If you use another writer's words without her knowledge or consent, you are at the very least in violation of some important requirements of professional courtesy. Whether the original author still "owns" her words or whether, on the contrary, they are in the public domain, so that the author's formal permission to republish is not required, can be a very difficult legal question, and it is easy to make an honest mistake in your attempt to answer it. But since you are not going to publish your college homework assignment, the problem does not even arise in your case. A general obligation to your readers, however, persists, as does the scholar's presumed devotion to the truth, and a duty to the original author (even if she is now dead and her works are legally considered public domain) to acknowledge her prior authorship. The way these obligations are discharged is by putting all of the words borrowed from another source in quotation marks. Whether the original passage was spoken, or written, whether it was available only handwritten or typed or printed, whether published or kept private, if it appears in your paper you must acknowledge the original writer's authorship. Part of the conventional method of doing this is to put all of the "borrowed words" in quotation marks.

If you have taken only a general idea or a logical argument from the original writer without taking her exact words, then it will be impossible to use quotation marks as a device for acknowledging your debt. Nevertheless, courtesy, accuracy, and simple honesty require that you acknowledge your borrowing. That can be done by attaching a numeral to the word in your text that is the beginning of your discussion of the borrowed point, or perhaps the last word of that discussion, and then corresponding to that numeral in the ordering of footnotes or endnotes, include a statement attributing the borrowed argument to its original source, and acknowledging its influence on your thought. Especially courteous language might also help make things go smoothly, but avoid flowery compliments. For example, the following idioms are frequently used: "I owe this point to Mary Moe, who first made it in her suggestive article, 'Ethical Relativism' in *Philosophical Review,* January, 1942, pp. 176–243"; *or* "I am indebted to Professor John Doe who first suggested this idea in his helpful volume, *Things* (Princeton, N.J.: Princeton University Press, 1960), pp. 1–94," *or* "This argument was first called to my attention in a discussion with George Goe, to whom I remain grateful," and so on. Of course if you have footnoted another writer in the text primarily as part of an argument against her views or for some other negative criticism, do not use such terms as "seminal" and "grateful" in your citation of her in the note. And of course it goes without saying that if you do not really believe an article has merit, do not say it does!

There are numerous reasons why the author of a book or an essay might wish to mention ("cite") other books or essays by herself or by others. She may have just quoted the other writer in the main body of her text, and she will now wish to acknowledge that person's authorship of the quoted passage. If the passage is three or more sentences long, it is customary to indent the entire passage without using quotation marks. By conventional understanding, the indenture itself indicates that the long indented passage is quoted, so that quotation marks are not needed. But if the passage is short—no more than three sentences long—it will be sufficient to leave it where it is in the main body of the text and place quotation marks in front of the first word and behind the last word of the quoted material. Thus one might write—

As Wittgenstein said, "Whereof one cannot speak, thereof one must be silent."[1]

The note number, in this case 1, is placed outside and above the terminal quotation marks. Then, either at the end of the article (endnote) or at the foot of the page (footnote) the corresponding numeral 1 appears, followed by the appropriate citation. In the case of the present example, you should further help the reader by providing a more detailed identification of the work from which the quotation is taken, so that the reader can order it from the publisher or locate it more expeditiously in the library stacks. To this end, an endnote or footnote citation will list (again) the quoted author's name (last name first) followed by a comma, the author's first name, and a period.[2] In our present illustration, the complete citation would be as follows:

Wittgenstein, Ludwig. *Tractatus Logico-Philosophicus,* trans. D.F. Pears and B.F. McGuinness (London: Routledge & Kegan Paul, 1961),

Note that this work was translated from another language (German), so the citation identifies the translators.

---

[2]I present just one of many ways that a footnote can be written. Some colleges and universities require their students to adhere to a particular style of footnoting. If your institution does have such a policy, you should, of course, follow that one.

In your citations, make sure that book titles and journal names are underlined or italicized. The titles of journal articles or book chapters, however, are to be in Roman type and not underlined in your manuscript.

ALTERNATIVE FORMATS FOR NOTES

As we have seen, some writers list their citations in footnotes, that is, in numerical order at the foot of each page, whereas others opt for endnotes, that is, all together in numerical order following the last line of the article. Neither method is clearly preferable. There is another option you will have that is more basic: that is the choice between two ways of using an endnote format. One can choose the traditional system, still preferred in the humanities fields including philosophy, and the system of parenthetical references and bibliographical reference lists, used mostly in the social sciences, to be explained below.

Kate L. Turabian, in her authoritative work on the subject,[3] maintains that notes have

> four main uses: (a) to cite the authority for statements in the text—
> specific facts or opinions as well as exact quotations, (b) to make
> crossreferences, (c) to make incidental comments upon, to amplify, or to
> qualify textual discussion—in short, to provide a place for material that
> the writer deems worthwhile to include but which would in the writer's
> judgment interrupt the flow of thought if introduced into the text, and
> (d) to make acknowledgments.

Notes of types (a) and (b) essentially involve citations of other writings, whereas types (c) and (d) are "incidental comments" that in most cases are made without reference to other scholarly materials. Some scholars are disturbed by what they take to be unnecessary inclusion amidst the citation notes of the so-called incidental or supplementary comments. The latter often seem to be digressive afterthoughts. One proposed change is to segregate the comment-notes by making them footnotes identified not by numerals but by asterisks and similar symbols, while reserving endnotes for numerically ordered citation notes.

This problem is solved in a different way by the system of citation now favored in social science fields. Comments of types (c) and (d) are included in footnotes or endnotes. But notes of types (a) and (b) are marked by parenthetical references within the text of the paper containing the author, publication date, and page number of the work cited. For instance, if your paper includes a direct quote, it will look like this—

---

[3]Turabian, Kate L. *A Manual for Writers,* 5th ed. (University of Chicago Press, 1987), p. 122.

**"Whereof one cannot speak, thereof one must be silent"
(Wittgenstein, 1960, p. 250).**

If the reader wants to have more information about this work of Wittgenstein's, she can look at your bibliography, a listing of all the works that you cite in your essay, which comes at the very end of your paper. The bibliography will contain full citations, which differ from the footnote format shown above by putting the date of publication in a more prominent place.

Wittgenstein, Ludwig. (1960). *Tractatus Logico-Philosophicus,* **trans. D.F. Pears and B.F. McGuinness. London: Routledge & Kegan Paul.**

The bibliography will list the citations for different authors alphabetically. If you cite more than one work by the same author, list them chronologically.

The aesthetic principle of parenthetical format is to include the bare minimum of relevant information. So, if you mention the name of the writer you mean to cite right at the point that you are citing him, you may include the publication date of the work and the page number only.

As Wittgenstein said, "Whereof one cannot speak, thereof one must be silent" (1960, p. 250).

If you have cause to reference multiple works from a single author that were written in the same year, this can be marked by adding a lower case letter to the parenthetical citation. For instance, your paper may include a passage like the following:

Jane Doe advocated a relativist moral theory at one point in her career (1994a). However, soon afterwards, she came to the conclusion that relativism is toppled by a devastating counterexample (1994b).

In your bibliography, Doe's works will be listed as follows:

Doe, Jane. (1994a). "Relativism Defended," *Journal of Ethical Inquiry,* **Vol. 27, No. 3. pp. 112–119.**
Doe, Jane. (1994b). "Relativism Refuted," *Journal of Ethical Inquiry,* **Vol. 27, No. 4. pp. 175–188.**

The parenthetical reference has much to recommend it, especially its economy and simplicity. It is considerably easier to learn than the classic systems of footnoting. However, footnoted citations are still more commonly used than parenthetical citations, so let's return to a review of the rules for such systems.

ACCEPTABLE ABBREVIATIONS IN NOTES

The use of abbreviations of Latin terms in endnotes and footnotes is a practice centuries old. Very few scholars today are as familiar with Latin as their predecessors were, but most have come to recognize the abbreviations in the writings of others. Prevailing judgments now tolerate the practice if it is confined to the notes themselves, kept out of the main text, and if it is restricted to the most commonly recognized and least arcane of the Latin expressions. This compromise helps today's writers by permitting them the savings of time and energy otherwise spent looking things up in Latin dictionaries, and provides the usual advantages of abbreviation—savings in time and energy. The following is a plausible but partial list of abbreviations for use especially in secondary use notes, as opposed to first appearance among the notes in a given article. If the first reference in a bibliography is spelled out fully, then subsequent references to the same work do not have to be spelled out in the same tedious fullness. The following secondary abbreviations are widely recognized and acceptable.

ca, short for *circa,* which means "about," "approximately"
cf. means compare (imperative)
e.g., short for *exempli gratia,* which means "for example"
et al., short for *et alii,* which means "and others"
ibid., short for *ibidem,* which means "in the same place"
i.e., short for *id est,* which means "that is"
infra, below
et passim, which means "and here and there"
loc. cit., short for *loco citato,* which means "in the place cited"
op. cit., short for *opere citato,* which means "in the work cited"
supra, which means "above"
trans., translated by
vol., volume (plural, "vols.")

Needing special explanation are the secondary footnote references *ibid., op. cit.,* and *loc. cit. Ibid.* is short for *ibidem,* which means "in the same place." Instead of two long-winded notes containing almost exactly the same words, you can write the wordy one first, and then substitute *"ibid."* What *"ibid."* means in effect is "in the same place as that mentioned in the immediately preceding note." Thus, the following notes would be correct in form:

[13]**Jones, Robert T. *Collected Absurdities* (New York: Oxford University Press, 1974), pp. 13–26.**
[14]*Ibid.*, **p. 28.**

Op. cit. is short for *opere citato,* which in Latin means "in the work cited." It is a way of referring to a citation earlier in a list of notes. If several references to the cited work have already been made, then "*op. cit.*" refers to the first one. Thus in a list of, say, 20 endnotes, there may be five citations of Jones's *Absurdity Compounded*. These could be worded as follows.

[13]**Jones, Robert T. *Absurdity Compounded* (New York: Oxford University Press, 1975), pp. 1–18.**
[14]***Ibid.*, p. 19.**
[15]***Ibid.*, p. 106.**
...
[17] **Jones, *op. cit.*, p. 92.**
...
[20] **Jones, *op. cit.* p. 93.**

The trouble with this system is that it does not always uniquely select out its reference. Footnote 13 above is precise and explicit. No abbreviations are used. Footnote 14 means "in the same place as that mentioned in footnote 13." Footnote 15 means "in the same place as that mentioned in footnotes 14 and 13." Footnote 17, however, may cause the reader some inconvenience. To get its full meaning, the reader must rummage among the earlier footnotes to find the first full and explicit reference to the Jones book, and that can be a long way back indeed. My own solution to the problem is as follows. Wherever I use *op. cit.*, I add the footnote number of its earliest explicit citation. Thus, I would word footnote 17 as follows:

[17]**Jones, *op. cit.* (see note 13), p. 92.**

That little addition (see note 13) enables the reader to go straight to note 13 where the full citation of the Jones book is located.

Loc. cit. is short for *loco citato*, which is Latin for "in the place cited." This is a phrase which in its typical use is more precise even than *ibid*. Suppose note 25 is to the first citation of the Jones book, and note 26 is *Ibid.*, p. 25. I intend note 27 to refer not just to "the work cited earlier," not even to the work cited in "the footnote immediately preceding this one" but rather to another sentence on the very *same page* as that cited in note 26. I can therefore write for note 27 simply *loc. cit.* with no further page number. If I had written *Ibid.*, I would be bound to add the page number again: *Ibid.*, p. 25. (*Loc. cit.* is simpler.)

3

Criteria for Grading Student Papers

What follows is a rough statement of one teacher's criteria for grading student papers in introductory philosophy classes.

CLARITY

The instructor, who must, in many universities, read as many as several hundred pages of student essays in a one- or two-week period, will have little patience for interpreting obscure, overblown, wordy, or rambling papers, however "profound" they may be. The very most important requirement in her view may be that the papers be written in simple lucid language, and that it be made apparent immediately to the reader exactly what the author is up to. To that end, the author should write a clear introductory paragraph stating exactly what he will attempt to do in the paper, and also a summary paragraph at the end reviewing the argument. It is often a good idea to write the introductory paragraph last. In that way, it is more likely to be an accurate "forecast" of what will follow.

A term paper will satisfy the requirement of clarity if the reader, when he has finished reading it, can answer easily and confidently the following three questions:

(i) What is the question the author has undertaken to answer (or the problem she has undertaken to solve)?

(ii) What is her answer (solution) to that question (problem)?

(iii) What reasons did she give in support of her answer (solution)?

The student should pose these three questions to herself before submitting her essay. Ideally, she should be able to pose her problem in a single interrogative sentence (for example "Are all human beings selfish?", "Is the mind identical with the brain?", "Is it rational to blame wrongdoers if their wrongful actions were predictable?"). Some good problems for papers might be mainly critical (for example, "Has Berkeley shown that what we are directly aware of in perception are our own sense-data?", "Do the arguments of Pascal or William James (either one or both) refute W.K. Clifford's account of 'the ethics of belief'?", "Does

17

Hume refute Paley's argument from design?"). The student should then be able to give her own answer, at least tentatively, in a single declarative sentence which will be the thesis of her paper, and she should be able to list her reasons, in outline, in a brief summary paragraph.

To whatever extent these questions are unanswered in the paper, in a form the reader can understand, the paper is obscure, and the most important criterion unsatisfied.

PRESENCE OF ARGUMENT

The thesis of a paper is the proposition it purports to establish, its conclusion, or the answer to its main question. The thesis plus the reasons given in its support (or the premises from which it is alleged to follow) are called an *argument*. A thesis without any supporting reasons is not an argument but rather a mere dogmatic statement of opinion. Do not write a "credo".[1] A simple statement of what you believe may be of biographical interest, but it can have no philosophical value. The point of a paper assignment in a philosophy course is to give the student some exercise in philosophical reasoning and argumentation, not to inform the instructor of the student's beliefs.

COGENCY OF ARGUMENT

It is not sufficient, of course, merely to offer considerations which purport to be reasons for the thesis. The reasons must in fact support the conclusion. They must be relevant and cogent. It may be impossible to state in the abstract general criteria of cogency. This is largely a matter of judgment and some disagreements among reasonable people may be difficult to resolve. That does not mean, however, that it is a mere "matter of opinion." If an argument violates a canon of deductive logic, then the instructor (who regards himself as an expert on such questions) will spot it as a *fallacy* (incorrect argument). Similarly, if the author tries to escape the responsibility to give reasons, by rhetoric, bombast, sententiousness, dogmatic reiteration, or pious homilies, this will quickly be spotted. A good argument is simply a set of considerations which lend weight or plausibility to the thesis, i.e. which create some presumption of its truth. A philosophy paper then need not be a rigorous demonstration or "proof " of its thesis, and would do well not to pose as such.

---

[1]The English word "credo" was a word in the ancient Latin language meaning "I believe." In modern English it still has a personal referent, namely the speaker or writer who uses it. It tends to be used now to mean the most basic or fundamental beliefs (plural) of the speaker or writer.

ORIGINALITY, SUBTLETY, IMAGINATIVENESS

It does not take very much talent to argue cogently for a thesis, just *any* thesis. One might actually prove an important though obvious thesis, quite conclusively, with little effort at all. Consider for example the following perfectly valid argument for a conclusion that I, for one, regard as important:

(i) All men are mortal.

(ii) Feinberg is a man.

(iii) Therefore, Feinberg is mortal.

The student whose thesis is that easy to prove has not shown much originality and deserves very little credit. The harder the task, the greater is the ingenuity required, and the credit to be gained. All arguments have to begin with assumptions, that is, with statements that function as reasons (premises) in the argument but are not themselves supported with still further reasons. Don't worry then if you discover important unsupported statements in your argument. But if your assumption is simply your conclusion in different wording, or if it is itself probably false or very implausible, or if it makes the task of supporting your conclusion far too *easy,* then it is ill-suited as an assumption. In your paper, you might very well announce what your crucial starting assumptions are. For example, you might write that you propose to examine utilitarian ethics from the point of view of a committed Christian. That might be an interesting and difficult undertaking. On the other hand, it would make things far too easy to assume the truth of Christianity in a refutation of atheism!

In order to give a good argument for a philosophical conclusion, it is necessary only to give *good reasons* in its support. It is not necessary to write an essay that resembles in its form an exercise in Euclidean geometry. It is not necessary to achieve or even to attempt to achieve mathematical rigor. Neither is it necessary to produce an argument whose outline resembles a demonstrative syllogism, that is an argument which shows that given certain reasonable assumptions that the reader might share, the conclusion you support must *necessarily* be true. Such an argument, if it works, is indeed a "good reason" for its conclusion, but if you aim for that kind of certainty you are likely to achieve it only at the price of triviality.

In any event, to argue with some cogency for a non obvious, non trivial conclusion will require both subtlety and imagination. There can be nothing routine or automatic about it, no easy formulas to apply. If your paper does argue with unusual subtlety and imagination, but does not quite succeed, it will be a better paper than one which succeeds "routinely" in a task that is too easy. A truly excellent student paper will also do well by the standard of originality. The concept of originality is not the same as the concept of novelty or innovation. Unless you are an extraordinary creative genius, you are not likely to think of something genuinely novel, something no one has ever thought of before. That would be too much to expect. But it is not too much to expect that your paper be original, that is that it have its place of origin in you, that it not be a mere copy of someone else.

DEGREE OF DIFFICULTY

There is no need to say much more about this criterion. It is a corollary of the criterion of originality stated above. The more original the argument, the greater the difficulty. There is obvious justice in rewarding the difficult achievement more than the easy one, other things being equal. That being so, we might say that subtlety and imagination are all part of one criterion with originality and difficulty.

The only problem with the originality-difficulty criterion is the practical task of applying it. There is no objective measure whose application to the paper is visible, public, and clear. Instead, when the student asks the professor why she didn't get a higher grade, the professor must sometimes explain that there was nothing conspicuously wrong with it, no logical fallacies, no glaring mistakes. Rather the paper was a bit pedestrian, ordinary, undistinguished, or the like. "How does one tell," responds the student, "that one's paper is pedestrian, not very creative, subtle or imaginative?" At this point the professor might be reduced to mumbling something about "intuition," which will suggest to the student a mystic trance during which the appropriate grade suddenly emerges in a flash of light. There is no need, however, to speak of "intuition." The more fitting word is "judgment": grading a paper for its positive virtues is one of the basic human activities that call for judgment, and whose aims cannot be achieved without it. It does not follow that there is no truth or falsity in such judgment, that one person's judgment is as good as another's, or that judgment is merely a form of prejudice in disguise. The judgments of some persons are better, or more accurate, than those of others. Most of us firmly believe that, which is why we disagree so strongly from time to time in our own judgments. The fact remains that we do disagree, and often about matters too subtle to be settled easily.

ORDERING THE CRITERIA

If there are four or five criteria applicable to student philosophy papers, depending on how we count them, in what order of importance do they stand? If a paper is obscure to the point of total unintelligibility, then it is no better than no paper at all, and that is about as bad as a paper can be. In that sense the criterion of clarity is the most "important." If a paper is quite clear, even well written and illustrated, but lacks an argument in support of its conclusion, it is a mere autobiographical "credo," and not a philosophical paper at all. In that sense, the criterion of having an argument is perhaps the second most important. Even a poor argument, for our purposes, is better than no argument at all. But a paper whose argument is so bad that it is *not* better than no argument at all would totally fail to satisfy the third criterion, which might in that sense be thought to be the third most important criterion. A paper that satisfies to some substantial degree the first three criteria will be a good paper indeed, perhaps worth the grade of B. But if it is pedestrian, unoriginal, not particularly distinguished, then it fails, perhaps totally, to satisfy the fourth criterion, degree of difficulty, which can be called perhaps the fourth most important. If degree of difficulty is not separated from originality as a distinct criterion, then it is the next most important. A paper that satisfied all the criteria including this one would be worthy of an A. Indeed, a paper would probably have to do well by all the criteria to be worth an A unless it did so well by one of them that it balanced a weak performance on one of the others.

If it is more "important" not to get a very bad grade than it is to get a very good one, then the criteria may be ranked in importance in the order indicated. But things are more complicated than that. Criterion 5 probably cannot be satisfied unless 1–4 are too, and criterion 4 cannot be satisfied unless 1–3 are also, and so on. Moreover "satisfaction of a criterion" is a matter of degree. Some may be fully satisfied, some barely satisfied at all. And to further complicate things, our initial assumption that it is more important not to do poorly than to do well can be, and will be, widely challenged.

4

General Principles
of Good Writing

CLARITY AGAIN

For all we know, a moderately unclear paper may reflect only the difficulty of the subject or the reader's unfamiliarity with it. Such a paper, no matter who is responsible for the obscurity, may yet convey something to its readers, just as a slightly out-of-focus photograph can do the same. A totally unclear paper, however, like a totally undeveloped photograph, conveys nothing at all to anyone. At its extreme, it is like a blank sheet of paper or an essay in Chinese or ancient Greek. To the reader who knows not a word of those languages, it will appear to be only black marks on a white page, signifying nothing.

Young writers are often advised to have a clear conception of the "audience" for whom they are writing, and which persons in that audience may be presumed to understand their comments, without strenuous efforts. The professor or her assistant who will read your paper has a big head start at learning philosophy, which is, in a way, like a "language" that most people know poorly if at all. If you consider people like your instructors to be your primary audience, you will risk seeming snobbish or patronizing to others. So write instead for an intelligent, reasonably well-educated adult—*any* such adult. Instead of writing for an audience of philosophy professors, write for the intelligent person who is as inexperienced and unread in philosophy as you are. Assume only that she speaks and understands English, and, like most normal people, is capable of becoming genuinely interested in philosophical problems.

No matter what sort of hypothetical audience your paper speaks to, however, it is important that it be intelligible to those persons, for otherwise your paper will be beyond the understanding of precisely the sort of reader you would like to reach. If you are to communicate at all, your prose must be intelligible; for your prose to be intelligible it must be clear; and the great enemy of clarity is wordiness. The way to avoid wordiness is to cultivate the basic communicative virtues—simplicity, directness, and economy.

SIMPLICITY

One obstacle to clarity is sheer quantitative complication. Long complex sentences that are likely to confuse all but the most patient readers do not at first mislead the person who composes them. She is living, for the moment, intensely in her own prose, and she thinks she knows where her writing is going, and what she wants it to say. But the ordinary reader, even a reasonable person in the hypothetical audience, will more easily lose his way. The professor who assigned the paper and/or her assistant, both of whom must now read a large pile of them, may lose their patience even quicker, take out their red pencils, and with them write, time and time again, "awkward" in the margins.

Sentences whose awkwardness is the result of excessive length and complication are very difficult for the author to discover while she is composing them or even at her first effort to read them. But if the author puts down her manuscript at the end of the day, and returns refreshed the next day, she may wonder how she ever came to compose such a monster. I find such sentences in my own first drafts every two or three pages.

There are many ways of remedying the situation. The simplest is to find a grammatical way of chopping the sentence into two. If the sentence is basically a conjunction of two independent clauses, each of which is qualified by several dependent clauses, you can replace the comma or semicolon that connects the independent clauses with a period that will separate them. Capitalize the next word and treat it as the first word of a new sentence.

Another way of improving "awkward sentences" is by measures of austere economy. Imagine that you were offered thousands of dollars by a publisher, but on the understanding that every time you use an additional word, $100 is deducted from your savings. In that frame of mind, run through the complex sentence in a verbicidal fury, striking every word that is not essential. Adjectives and adjectival phrases are the most likely to be inessential. For example:

✧[1] **He looked very strong and powerful, seated there, in the room, on a chair.**

The word "very" is often a plausible target of the pruning knife. Sometimes the cause of the reader's confusion is simply that one of the subordinate clauses, though worded correctly, is badly placed in the sentence so that the reader proceeds to a switching point and then inadvertently takes the wrong track in a direction other than that in which the author intended him to go. To follow up this railroad metaphor, it is as though a railway switchman has failed to pull a switch so that when the reader's attention gets to the switching point, it proceeds down a new track ending up in complete confusion. Sometimes I find that by moving words around, I can easily correct the situation. I can draw a circle around a phrase, perhaps around three words, perhaps ten, and move the words in the circle to a new place, perhaps earlier in the sentence.

---

[1]Throughout this book wherever a sentence is used as an example of poor writing I use the symbol ✧. Samples of writing that are correct and proper are preceded by a solid circle—•.

ECONOMY

Often the student who has the most to learn about writing is a "verbal type" with a natural gift for gab. Words come flowing in torrents from her mouth, her pen, or her computer. They are good words, imaginatively combined in colorful metaphors. Many of them are precise words, well-selected to make her point. Then synonyms or near-synonyms make the point again. Other words add nothing to what is asserted but fancied adornment. Where the writer has been unable to make up her mind between two descriptions, she has used them both. Rewording can always be done later, she tells herself, "it is so easy with a computer." The student in this example is potentially a superb writer. Yet her writing at this moment is poor. All her papers exhibit the same fault; they are overwritten. The writer's flaw that undermines her writing despite her own great aptitude is lack of self-discipline.

I have often resorted to a dramatic technique for helping a student improve his self-discipline. I will rewrite a page of his paper reducing, wherever possible, its wordiness. Adjectives and adverbs that are dear to him get slashed in the process, as I emit whoops of pleasure. Whole phrases, even some whole clauses, are deleted. Sometimes I do this by maneuvering sentence components into a different order so that one can see more clearly which are inessential. Then out they come. The student-author by now has caught the spirit and joins the fun. One of us cuts while the other one counts. The one who counts places a numeral in the margin, circles it, and places a plus or minus (usually minus) sign in front of it. Then at the end of a page, we tally up the score. How many words have been cut in the rewriting? Frequently the net change comes to a hundred or more, and the prose is spare and plain, no chore at all to read.

I too have to control my wordiness, just as a person prone to obesity must watch his calories. In the first draft of this chapter, for example, the opening sentence read as follows:

♦ **Clarity. For all we can know, a moderately unclear paper may reflect only the difficulty of the subject or the reader's (grader's) own unfamiliarity with the experience of the writer when the writer has presumed in him a background that he does not in fact have.**

That was much too wordy. In the printed version that you are now reading the word total is 23. The original draft, which I threw out, contained 46. So in the final version, the word total is cut in half, and what remains is much better written to boot.

PADDING

Prominent among overwritten papers are those that are excessive in a particular way. They seem to be almost deliberately packed with trivia and irrelevancies. The reader cannot help but suspect that the author overwrites because he has very little to say about the assigned topic, and is trying to conceal that fact by filling up the space with background, asides, irrelevant digressions, and so on. When the grader is given a student paper that is less than one page long, she need not be very fresh and alert to see that the assigned topic has been inadequately treated. When the student adds a comment about "prehistoric man," or Chinese social systems, or about the views of a minor Renaissance philosopher about a different subject, or when he adds a quarter of an inch to the side margin on each page, the total number of pages concerned with the assigned topic may remain less than one, but there may be six or eight pages submitted, because of the expansive effect of "padding." But though students often try this maneuver, the grader is almost never swindled. Padding, of course, is a matter of degree and can be done with more subtlety and to a lesser extent. Wherever and however it occurs, it is almost as much a flaw as blank pages in a manuscript would be.

The most common place where padding is found in a student paper is in the opening paragraph. Avoid constructing first sentences that share a common form with the following example:

⬧ **Ever since the time of the cave men philosophers have been asking whether mind and body are the same thing.**

There are often reasons, however, to think that such openings, when restricted to the first paragraph or two, are not *deliberate* padding, though padding they indubitably are. They may very well be the result of the student's use of a strategy like the one recommended in Chapter 1 for overcoming a writing block. The student built up his momentum by dashing off some conventional trivialities that got him started, and then perhaps, by the time his first draft was completed, he forgot to delete it.

REPETITIVENESS

Not all repetitiveness is classifiable as wordiness. A writer's prose may be lean and sinewy with no tendency to use too many words to make her points, and yet she makes the same point, and makes it well, over and over again. Why do some writers keep repeating themselves this way? The most common cause, I suspect, is insecurity about whether their point is getting across. Just as in ordinary spoken conversation, one party may be unsure of her partner's ability to follow her meaning, or she may lack confidence in her own ability to do justice to the subtlety of her point. Within limits, a certain amount of repetitiveness might be a good thing. If the point you are trying to make is indeed a difficult one, it will not hurt first to express it this way and then that way. An example or two might also assist communication. One's prose can be altogether too lean. Among beginning student philosophy papers, however, more seem to err on the side of excess than that of deficiency. So beware the greater danger.

REDUNDANCY

Not all writing mistakes consist of quantitative excess. Some rules for good writing rule out various forms of wordiness, though as we have already seen, others of them do not. But other writing errors consist not in the use of too many words, so much as the wrong word in the context. It is important for the student to understand that whether the error consists in using too many words or using the wrong sorts of words, the point of the rule against it is to protect the reader (and the writer too) from misunderstanding, confusion, boredom, sleepiness, and other unhappy states of mind. The same is true of the rules of punctuation, spelling, syntax, and diction. What grammarians call "redundancy" is a case in point. Like rust on neglected machinery, redundancy can appear anywhere. Probably because the Norman French conquered Anglo-Saxon England in 1066 and lived among the people they had conquered, the vocabulary of the English language was doubled and we English speakers have an extraordinary number of pairs of terms that are often joined together and used redundantly. How often have you heard politicians, when they have occasion to use the word "moral," add the words "and ethical" as if that rather close synonym of "moral" were part of a single word with it.

✧ **What this country needs is respect for moral and ethical standards.**

If you delete "and ethical," you will preserve sense and reduce wordiness, if only by two words. That is not much, but it is a start. If your paper has two or three such pairs per page, as some beginning student papers do, then it will seem cluttered and difficult to read. Other examples include "each and every," "first and foremost," and "to all intents and purposes." In other examples there are no artificial linkages of pairs, but an adjective repeats some part of the meaning of the noun it modifies. Advertisements frequently offer to make their customers "free gifts," and writers as well as legal witnesses are often urged to give the "true facts." Again, deleting the extra word will prevent one little bit of wordiness and create one small increase of readability.

27

MISPLACED EMPHASIS

Errors of wordiness distort communication indirectly by producing a littered linguistic landscape, which tires and distracts the reader. Other sorts of writing mistakes, however, mislead the reader quite directly, leading her eyes down a path other than that intended by the author. The reader then has to back up until she finds the point where she went off the track, return, and start over. The rule against misplaced emphasis is a good example of protection of the reader from transmission of the wrong message or else the failure to communicate altogether. Joseph M. Williams, in his valuable book *Style*,[2] provides an example:

✧ **No one can explain why that first primeval superatom exploded and thereby created the universe in a few words.**

I submit that any of us might compose a sentence like that one in our first hastily written draft. And any of us would quickly discover the error upon reading through it. The author intends to give emphasis to a point about the primordial explosion. The way to leave emphasis in the intended place is to stress the important words by placing them near the end of the sentence. And one way to do that, as Professor Williams advises, is to move the unimportant words ("in a few words") that are in the stressed place. In general we should move the more important information to the right or the less important to the left. The best way to reword the example is as follows:

• **No one can explain, in a few words, why that first primeval superatom exploded and thereby created the universe.**

The original sentence may have suggested to some readers what presumably was not in the author's mind, namely that the sentence was about the "few words"— "Let there be light."

PRETENTIOUSNESS AND FANCY WORDS

The rule warning against fancy and pretentious words follows from the general policy of seeking simplicity discussed earlier. "Fancy words" are not as simple as they might be. In fact, almost all the fancy words have near-synonyms that are less fancy. Unless turgidity and multisyllabic constructions are taken to be virtues in special contexts, they would appear to be flaws. In the first place, not every reader will know what such words mean, so the writer's goal of communication might often be defeated. In the second place, the motive for using words that are in large part unknown is sometimes affectation, or at least so it is often perceived.

---

[2]Williams, John M. *Style: Toward Clarity and Grace* (Chicago: University of Chicago Press, 1990), pp. 68–69.

Affectation is a kind of snobbery—a peculiarly unpleasant character flaw. A related motive is to make a simple idea seem more impressive—a kind of false speaking akin to misrepresentation.[3] I suppose that one can claim that morally offensive writing might still be good writing by the morally neutral standards we use for judging literary merit. But that would be to overlook the fatiguing, distracting, and irritating effects of pompous language on the reader and their interference with quick and accurate comprehension.

The following are objectionably pompous words (mostly from the Latin) as paired with a simpler synonym (mostly Anglo-Saxon).

✧ Example of big verbs	• Corresponding simpler word
to endeavor	to try
to utilize	to use
to facilitate	to bring about
to implement	to put into effect
to effectuate	to make effective

None of these words are specially invented technical terms referring to some esoteric subject matter. The meanings captured in the simpler synonyms are really quite ordinary.

Another motive for terminology that I find pompous (but one which is perhaps more understandable) is to lend respectability to the official language of professional groups like policemen, social workers, physicians, nurses, even barbers. Williams gives a typical example, one that deserves to be a classic:

✧ **This impulse toward an elevated diction has proved quite durable; it accounts for the difference today between 'The adolescents who had effectuated forcible entry into the domicile were apprehended' and 'We caught the kids who broke into the house.'**[4]

Judged by ordinary standards, the fancier specimen is terrible writing. But then police are no doubt fond of it insofar as it creates a public attitude toward them that is similar to that which already exists toward doctors and lawyers.

---

[3]Michael Crichton, on the language of medicine from *New England Journal of Medicine*, as quoted in Williams, *op. cit.* (see note 2), p. 10.

[4]Williams, *op. cit.* (see note 2), p. 7.

A MISCELLANY OF FURTHER JUDGMENTS

(i)   Avoid patronizing the reader by unnecessary explanation.

(ii) Avoid preachiness. (Then look up "sententiousness," and avoid *it* too.)

(iii) Avoid inappropriate dogmatism. Use "perhaps," "often," "sometimes," "most," "many"—terms that soften an otherwise dogmatic tone.

(iv) Avoid excessive "victory claims," for example, "I have succeeded in proving what others have doubted for centuries!"

(v)   Avoid "fighting words" such as "absurd," "stupid," "ridiculous," as applied, of course, to others.

(vi) Do not quote "authority" for a philosophical conclusion as a substitute for argument, as if its truth were a matter of empirical fact to which only experts have access.

(vii) Do not make excuses in the text of the paper, for example:

✧ **I am a mere college freshman, and this is hard for me.**

(viii) Avoid making pompous statements about "man." Even in biology it is no longer appropriate to use the masculine specific word as the name of a whole biological species. There are plenty of other words available that are less objectionable: "humanity," "human beings," "men and women," "humankind," and so on. Especially avoid such statements as

✧ **Man has always wondered whether ethical egoism is true.**

Even if there were no other objection to "man" as the name of our entire biological species, there would be objection to this kind of generalization. So, for example, if we were to substitute (say) "Humankind has always wondered..." we would have a sentence of the form "Every normal human being has always wondered ... ," and one can expect virtually every philosophical statement of that form to be false.

(ix) Do not write "I feel that . . ." For example, do not write

✧ **I feel that materialism is the best solution to the mind-body problem.**

Deep authentic emotion deserves our respect, but it does not belong in a philosophy paper. If you use "feel" as a synonym of "believe," you should consult the list of near synonyms for "believe" that I have compiled below, page 76.

5

Mistakes of Grammar

GRAMMATICAL AND NONGRAMMATICAL WRITING ERRORS

In a recent western historical magazine, there appears the following sentence:

⟡ **Later, the old cowboy who owned the horse and his girlfriend invited us to spend the night in their trailer.**

When I got to the point in the article where the quoted sentence occurred, my mind left the track and I had to go back to the beginning and start over, if the article were to continue to make sense to me. For a moment, I thought that the old cowboy "owned" not only "the horse," but his "girlfriend." Then for a moment I thought the girlfriend was the horse's (perhaps he was a colt and she a filly?). Then very quickly I tried the remaining interpretation and it worked. But I had been slowed down for just a moment because the way the author had placed his words created possible interpretations that misrepresented his own intentions.

The author of the quoted sentence violated no rule of grammar or diction. What he did was no "federal offense." But he did confuse at least one reader, and that is not what good prose writing is supposed to do. I make this kind of nameless writing error at least once every two or three pages in the first draft of everything I write. What causes the mistake is the writer's hurry and consequent inattention. As ideas come to me, I get excited and write furiously, not stopping to try alternative locations in the sentence for single words or phrases that seem to have become lost. But in my second draft, which is largely just a rewriting of difficult parts of the first draft, I make the needed clarifications. There are two things to say about the corrective process. First, it is surprisingly difficult sometimes to rephrase such sentences. The best I could do with the sentence about the old cowboy was as follows:

• **Later the old cowboy who owned the horse invited us to spend the night with him and his girlfriend in their trailer.**

My second impression about this and similar examples is that they are the most frequent writing errors among good writers, and facility at rewriting them is one of the best tests we have of writing ability. Perhaps the main difference between "errors of placement" (my proposed name for them) and mistakes of grammar is that the latter can be interpreted as violations of readily formulable *rules,* whereas the former cannot.

CRITERIA OF CORRECT GRAMMAR

Writing essays is a form of activity that is governed by its own rules, but it is often unclear what the relevant rule is, how it is to be interpreted, how wellgrounded it is, or from whence comes its claimed authority. Those critics who claim to speak with authority on such matters are in frequent disagreement about what a correct rule prescribes. Some authorities try to be democratic, tolerant, and permissive. Others are called (usually by their opponents) elitists, purists, or conservatives. The permissive school claims that the actual usage of English language speakers, or a strong consensus among them, determines whether a given word or phrase is used correctly. The permissive critic is likely to argue that it cannot be right to squelch a speaker's spontaneity without good reason. If a given rule can be violated without noticeable consequence, with no odd sound to the ear, no jarring distraction, no departure from customary usage, then, in the permissive view, it is not reasonable simply to condemn it as "incorrect." The more conservative critic will stress the interest we all share in slowing linguistic change and preserving stability so that there will be a minimum of miscommunication.

The permissive critic, depending on exactly how permissive she is, will justify grammatical rules by appealing to a consensus of English speakers. Such a consensus can consist of any one of three different kinds of groupings. The widest such justifying consensus would be that consisting of the habits of usage of a consensus of English speakers. The second sort of appeal could be to a consensus of *educated* (thus specially qualified) English speakers. The third sort of appeal would be to the consensus of the *best writers* of English, both now and in the past.

The most commonly held view these days is that the consensus of *educated* writers and speakers of English is the appropriate consensus to use in determining grammatical correctness. This view of the matter is an apparent compromise between the permissiveness of the liberal critic who treats all speakers of a given language alike without class distinction and the more purist scholar who insists on the importance of educated usage. This formulation has satisfied a larger number of scholars than the more democratic appeal to a consensus that includes almost everyone. Moreover, it has seemed to many scholars that limiting membership in the relevant consensus to specially qualified language users can provide a way of grounding grammatical corrections in objectively rational considerations. The restriction to specially qualified persons makes an appeal not just to how people— any people—do in fact talk but also to the reasons (other than self-centered personal advancement) *why* they talk and write that way. If all and only educated people speak in a certain manner, perhaps that is because, being educated, they have been made aware of certain other reasons for speaking and writing the way they do. In that case, it is the educated person's *reasons* for talking as she does that justify the rules, not the fact of her being educated, alone.

An examination of the educated person's reasons for observing standard grammatical rules, may, however, turn up incentives of a sort less likely to suggest "objective rationality." In many countries, our own included, how one speaks and writes reveals not only her geographical place of residence and ethnic background, but also her degree of education and general intellectual credentials. Correct grammar might even determine one's eventual membership in a higher social class and the economic benefits that go with it.

The conservative "purist" often seeks a way of justifying rules that will reveal their inherent rationality, as opposed to the arbitrariness that characterizes some of our traffic rules. American motorists drive on the right side of the road, not because there is any inherent superiority in right over left, but because it is essential that everyone do the same thing if we are to avoid collisions. Rules of grammar, in the view of purists, are not like that. There *is* an inherently superior rationality, they think, in saying "whom" rather than "who" in some contexts. This rationality, however, is not a matter of *logic,* as we shall see, since there is no logical contradiction in alternative rules of grammar.

Purists are less ready than their rivals to find exceptions to our established rules. There is class of grammatical rules, however, that even the most permissive liberals would hold to be nearly exceptionless. Almost every native speaker knows these rules. Few people ever have to deliberate in deciding whether or not to observe them. And their violation offends the ear by its very sound. These rules, in fact, help define what standard English is. Speakers of standard English *never* say:

✧ **Me and my friend done that already, irregardless of what I ain't yet said nohow.**

(I shall continue to use the diamond marker symbol—✧—to introduce statements that illustrate writing errors of all kinds.)

If such a sentence were part of a college student's philosophy paper, his teacher, no doubt, would ask him how long he has been living in this country, or whether he had graduated from what used to be called "grammar school." Such errors are not interesting for our present purposes, and not controversial, even though critics do disagree about whether the rules defining standard English have an inherent rationality to them or whether they are linguistic analogues of the "rule of the road" that requires motorists in America to drive in the right lane.

The third possible interpretation of "consensus" to which the permissive (or "liberal") critic might appeal makes an even greater concession to the purist (or "conservative") critic. From the openly democratic and the qualifiedly democratic criteria we have discussed thus far, we move now to those writers who propose a frankly meritarian criterion, namely that what justifies rules of correct grammar is the historic fact that the most skilled writers, those whose work has become a standard for the rest of us through the sheer force of its excellence, have consistently written in accordance with it, and have never in their roles as critics rejected it. In a way this criterion too appeals to a kind critical consensus, namely the consensus of "experts"—mostly professors critics, and editors—who identify the great writers whose own writings, in effect, support the grammatical rules in question. This appeal ultimately is not just to usage but the usage of the best writers as selected by the best critics.

In the next section of this chapter, I have listed a number of word-uses that have become the subject of grammatical rules. Those rules that I respect, I cautiously endorse, while remaining aware that there may be many permissible exceptions even to a good rule of grammar. Other rules have outlived their utility if they ever had any. Some are complicated, essentially sound, and easily illustrated in central cases, but puzzling in their application to the borderline cases.

A SAMPLER OF GRAMMATICAL RULES
AND THEIR PROBLEMS

The following discussion examines the way in which more or less settled rules of English grammar yield judgments of grammatical correctness or incorrectness in various sorts of writing situations. The judgments of my own on each sample predict the response that could be expected from a textbook editor or a professor, especially when they are the same person.

(1) *The vanishing apostrophe.* There are few grammatical rules simpler than that which governs the use of this punctuation symbol, and only the period (.) takes less ink to print. And yet that little piece of punctuation is now so commonly unused or misused that an American Professor of English was recently moved to contribute an article to *Newsweek* magazine complaining that it is rapidly disappearing from the language.[1] The apostrophe has two uses: to signal a contraction and to indicate that a word is being used in the possessive case. It is therefore ungrammatical to put an apostrophe where it does neither of those jobs or to omit putting it where it is needed to do one or another of them.

✧ **Professor Quine is thought by some to be this countrys leading philosopher.**

An apostrophe belongs between the letter "y" and the letter "s" in "countrys." This is needed to show that it is a possessive.

---

[1]Larson, Charles R. "It's Academic or Is It?", *Newsweek,* November 6, 1995.

✧ I simply cant understand.

An apostrophe should appear between the letter "n" and the letter "t." The contraction in this case speeds up the reading, and avoids the ambiguity caused by the fact that "cant" (without the apostrophe) has as many as four other meanings, including "the private language of the underworld" and "the insincere use of pious words."

✧ Hes not lost his hat, hes lost his brains'.

Here the writer has compounded his offense by placing an apostrophe where it does not belong, and omitting an apostrophe where it is needed. She tries to contract "He is," but succeeds only in creating an extraordinarily "uglisome"[2] merging of the two words, and twice at that. Then in aggravation of the offense she inserts an apostrophe at the very end after the plural word "brains," though neither possession nor contraction is part of her intention. A punctilious reader could waste several minutes puzzling over this.

✧ It's high price shocked me.

Here the writer should have written "Its" in place of "It's." "It's" is a contraction of "it is." The word "it" is a pronoun, like "him" and "her." The possessive form for pronouns is not indicated with an apostrophe. (An object belonging to him is his, not "him's.") The possessive form of "it" is spelled "its." Since many find all of this difficult to remember, it may be more helpful to reason that contractions must always be indicated with an apostrophe. So, by process of elimination, "its" is the spelling indicating possession.

As we have said, for most nouns the possessive is created by adding an apostrophe and an "s", but it is tricky when the noun ends in the letter "s" already, or when the noun, being plural, already ends in "s."

✧ Merchant's profits on this item are minimal.

✧ We are doing it for the girls' sake.

Both of these examples are incorrect if we make certain assumptions about the writer's intentions. If the writer is talking about the plurality, merchants, and the profitability their business possesses, then he should have placed the apostrophe after the "s" to indicate the plural possessive. In the second example, if the writer means to be saying something about a single particular girl, say his daughter, he should place the apostrophe between the "l" and the "s" in "girl's" to indicate the singular possessive. If, however, the writer meant to refer to multiple girls, the example is correct.

---

[2] *Loc. cit.*

Finally, some common nouns that do not end in "s" but have an "s" sound at the end are made possessive simply by adding the apostrophe, as in "for conscience' sake." Thus it is a mistake to write,

✧ **... for conscience's sake . . .**

or

✧ **... for consciences' sake . . .**

The rules applied in these examples are aids to the reader and the writer both. It is not errant pedantry for a copy-editor at a publishing house or a philosophy professor to insist that writing under review conform to them.

(2) *Ain't misbehavin'.* The word "ain't," oddly enough, has become virtually the standard example of a type of grammatical incorrectness, and also of a word whose disallowance is wholly arbitrary, without any support from utility or rationality. Proscription of this word by grammarians is traditional and customary. The proscribed words, actually a contraction of "am not," makes it possible to say some things that we do often wish to say, and to say them with less awkwardness than we create without those words. And yet everyone who knows English knows that this first person contraction is a no-no in formal contexts, useful and economical though it may be. In fact its unacceptability is part of the test by which we distinguish standard from non-standard English.

✧ **I am talented at grammar, ain't I?**

There is really no nonarbitrary objection to this use of a traditional verbal form in the first person. It seems just as reasonable as "am I not?" which is quite respectable.

• **I am talented at grammar, am I not?**

The acceptable form "am I not?" actually is a little more cumbersome, if it differs at all from "ain't I?" Here the acceptable form requires three separate sounds—(1) am, (2) I, (3) not, whereas the banished idiom requires only two— (1) ain't and (2) I.

Unlike the examples of first person usage, the samples of second and third person uses of "ain't" are more plausibly objectionable. Thus,

✧ **You're pretty smart, ain't you?**

and

✧ **She's very pretty, ain't she?**

use an archaic (first person) contraction to do the job reserved for second and third person pronouns. This would be as baffling as to say—

✧ **She's very pretty, am I not?**

It would also be bizarre to say, as some still do in a rather desperate attempt to bypass the restriction against "ain't"—

✧ **I am very creative, aren't I?**

which is an actually common use of second and third person pronouns to say something about oneself (the grammatical "first person"). There is no good reason to resort to this awkward and unpleasant idiom, since "am I not?" is an acceptable way of saying the same thing. Indeed, proper English speakers might even be well advised, in some contexts, to fall back on the French "*n'est-ce pas*"? But if they do, they must be prepared to forgive critics who will remind them that resorting to French will strike many readers as pretentious. And responding to a sentence like

✧ **I am very learned and sophisticated, *n'est-ce pas?***

those readers will be right.

(3) *Between or among?*   The rule here is quite simple and at first sight, if we are to have a rule at all, this is a sensible one. But like many other subtle grammatical rules, this one is violated almost as often as it is followed, even by well-educated and skilled writers. It does not pass the "ear test" by very much. That is, it does not strike the ear oddly, as (say) "Him and me worked together" does. In fact it may at this time be evolving its way out of existence. Nonetheless it is still strongly enough represented in usage, especially educated usage, that you can expect your teacher to urge its acceptance. It is not because of some superior rationality, however, that their recommendation is a good one, but rather because it is sufficiently entrenched in usage to cause confusion when violated. And there may even be some contexts in which departure from the rule subtly changes the meaning of a sentence.

The rule itself is simply stated. If you are writing about a relationship between two things, then you use, as I just did, the word "between," but if a relationship connects more than two things, then "among" is the preferred preposition. Thus,

- **World War II was a conflict among many countries, though in military terms it was primarily between Germany and the Soviet Union.**

✧ **There was a strong competition between many companies.**

✧ **A love affair broke out among Robert and Shirley.**

These latter two examples turn the rule upside down. Probably, therefore, they would be stricken from a term paper by a conscientious and literal-minded teacher, even though the rule that he would thereby be enforcing was called a "superstition" by its leading interpreters, H.W. Fowler and Sir

Ernest Gowers.[3] These famous scholars do not exactly display a reverence toward this and other grammatical rules. Indeed they quote, with approval, from the *Oxford English Dictionary,* first edition:

> In all senses, 'between' has been from its earliest appearances, extended to more than two.... It is still the only word available to express the relation of a thing to many surrounding things severally and individually; 'among' expresses a relationship to them collectively and vaguely: We should not say 'the space lying among three Powers.' But the superstition dies hard.

If, then, your professor criticizes your incorrect use of "among" and "between," do not give her a hard time. Accept her judgment, however, so that you might be agreeable, not out of a fancied "rational conviction" of the rule's inherent superiority.

(4) *Conjunctions as first words.* Some grammarians refer to the "rule" that one must never begin a sentence with "And" or "But." The argument in support of this rule is that conjunctions have been assigned the job of connecting two independent clauses in one sentence, so that when they are used to start sentences that need no tight connection to what preceded them, they are trespassing on the territory of other "constructions." We already have the "Period/capital letter/new sentence" device and the independent clause conjoiners for such jobs. Why mix them up? The answer, I think, is that this new assignment for a word that had a clear and important job of its own to do actually increases the writer's options. She can write longer and shorter sentences, mix them up, control rhythms, and the like, in more ways than were ever available before. So there is no unique rationality, no "case in logic" for this rule either. Further, the case in usage here is much weaker than that claimed in our earlier examples. As Williams points out, "Just about any highly regarded writer of nonfictional prose begins sentences with 'And' and 'But,' some more than once a page."[4] Gowers calls the rule against first word conjunctions "a faintly lingering superstition."[5] It is clear that on grounds of usage, indeed the usage of the most highly regarded writers, this rule is not supportable. If you are a peaceful soul, not inclined toward disputes, give in again to your professor, but in this case there is no reason beyond pure politeness for doing what she says.

(5) *Ungrammatical danglers.* "Dangling" is something that can happen to any kind of modifying phrase in English but perhaps most notoriously to those words called "participles." The best examples of dangling participles are irresistibly funny, so it is perhaps no wonder that isolated scholars in dusty libraries are often heard cackling with uncontrolled glee. It is also no

---

[3]Fowler, H.W. and Gowers, Sir Ernest. *Modern English Usage,* 2nd ed. (New York and Oxford: Oxford University Press, 1965), p. 708.

[4]Williams, Joseph M. *Style: Toward Clarity and Grace* (Chicago and London: University of Chicago Press, 1990), p. 182.

[5]Fowler and Gowers, *op. cit.* (see note 3), p. 29.

wonder that uses of constructions that are that comic embody some sort of grammatical mistake. Otherwise how could things go so hilariously wrong? Strunk and White give three examples.[6]

✧ **Being in a dilapidated condition, I was able to buy the house very cheap.**

✧ **Wondering irresolutely what to do next, the clock struck twelve.**

✧ **As a mother of five, my ironing board is always up.**

Nonparticipial danglers are also off track and comic. A modifier dangles, Williams tells us, "when its implied ['implied' by its location in the sentence] subject differs from the specific subject of the clause that follows it," and gives the following example:

✧ **Resuming negotiations after a break of several days, the same issues confronted both the union and the company.**[7]

A person, as reported by this sentence, does some action. The grammatical subject of that action is the group of flesh and blood human beings with the power or authority to do it, namely union and company leaders. The word in the sentence that stands in the place where the human subjects would most naturally be expected is a set of impersonal abstractions, namely "issues," or more precisely, "the same issues." Their "confronting" was not a kind of doing or acting. But the word order here suggests that the main kind of doing reported by the sentence was that "done" by these abstractions.

After an amused chuckle, the author of these words could easily rewrite the sentence by moving the two subjects into less misleading locations. Williams rewords the sentence as follows:

• **Resuming negotiations after a break of several days, the union and the company confronted the same issues.**[8]

Rewriting sentences that have dangling phrases is perhaps as good a writing exercise as one could hope to find. Moreover, it would give one a sense of appreciation of that set of grammatical rules requiring "agreement," those whose violation can lead to comical failures of communication. In the application of these rules there can be no quarreling with professors and critics. These rules obviously have a rational point well beyond mere "usage."

---

[6]White, E.B. and Strunk, William, Jr. *The Elements of Style*, second ed. (New York: The Macmillan Company, 1972), p. 9.

[7]Williams, *op. cit.* (see note 4), p. 148.

[8]*Loc. cit.*

(6) *The problem of sexist pronouns: some proposed solutions.* Suppose that a person is speaking very generally about *all people* rather than just women or just men, and that he expresses the democratic judgment that all of them should be free to choose their own self-fulfillment as they see fit. How should this commendable sentiment be voiced?

◇ **Each person should do his own thing.**

Until recently this formulation was considered, even by women, to be perfectly satisfactory. But with the advent of feminism, its flaws have become steadily more apparent. In English, wherever gender was in doubt, or the composition of a group was unknown, rules of grammar supported the presumption that males in the group, if any, have a priority. In Romance languages, the combination of one male and dozens of females makes the resulting aggregate male, so that the masculine pronoun applies to it. In recent years many women have pointed out the unfortunate effect on self-image and self-esteem of rules that seemed always to give priority to men over women. I therefore endorse the feminist position on this question and reject the formulation above that seems always to give priority to men. A second possibility is the following:

◇ **Each person should do her own thing.**

This would appear, at least at first, to be a mistake equal and opposite to the first one. Maybe it is only fair to give women the "unfair advantage" after a masculine monopoly over the centuries. Indeed perfect equality might justify using this feminine priority formulation for a century or two and then reverting to the masculine monopoly principle for the next couple of centuries, or perhaps alternating for a period of years rather than centuries until inequities have balanced out. But clearly this is the most cumbersome of all the possible solutions to our problem. This change would have special problems during the transition between the old and new ways. Every time a feminine pronoun were given priority it would be a conspicuous eye-catcher, distracting the attention of the reader from the subject the writer is talking about.

◇ **Each person should do his or her own thing.**

This is a moral improvement but a stylistic infelicity. The gain comes at high cost to the smoothness of the verbal flow. And when you mix the recommended gender alternation with an already complicated sentence, one that has two or more independent clauses, each of which has more than one dependent clause, and whose subject matter contains references to numerous people, male and female, in various complicated relationships with one another, the sentence can become ludicrous and unreadable.

A fourth attempt to solve the sexist pronoun problem displeases me, but I must acknowledge that it is steadily gaining, even among the educated, and seems destined to win out in the end. I refer to the solution that jettisons the long-established rule requiring agreement in number between a pronoun and its antecedent (the words it stands in for). I admit that agreement-rules are not rules of logic and not uniquely rational, but their violation produces an especially ugly sort of asymmetry that has for decades been avoided by our better writers, and taken as a sign of inadequate education by others. For that reason I classify the following as a grammatical error:

✧ **Each person should do their own thing.**

Not only is this "ugly"; it can also confuse a careful reader who is led by the plural pronoun to look for a plural subject, for whom she will look in vain. Since my reaction to this usage, once the general response of educated people, is now shared by fewer and fewer speakers, I have a grudging tolerance for this construction. Still, this usage, however convenient in spoken English, remains inappropriate in written English. Shortcuts that make sense in conversation can be incorrect when written, because of the expectation that an author will have the opportunity to rewrite and correct grammatical errors. Since this qualifies as such an error, I will always refrain from using it in my own writings.

The first four attempts, then, to solve the problem of "sexist pronouns," are in my view, failures. I reject or find flawed "his," "her," "his or her," and "their" (with a singular subject). By my reckoning, that leaves three other formulations, and I find each of these a satisfactory solution to the sexist pronoun problem. The first is the all-plural formulation:

• **All persons should do their own thing.**

Here the plural pronoun agrees with a plural subject and all is harmony. Second, we could write that—

• **One should do one's own thing.**

This is perfectly satisfactory too. One word of caution, however. Do not match the genderless "one" with the masculine "he"—a common mistake.

✧ **In this job one never knows when he will encounter a dangerous criminal.**

A less common mistake, though a mistake nonetheless, is to match "one" with "she."

✧ **If one wants to be healthy, she will exercise frequently.**

The third and final adequate solution to the problem of gendered pronouns is to use only one of them at a time for extended sections of the essay or book, and then at a later point switch to the other gender and use it exclusively for a while. This final technique will threaten to slow down your writing and lead you to forget where you are going *if* you try to combine it with first draft composition. So it might be better to do it after finishing a first draft. My own practice is to alternate randomly "she" or "her" with "he" or "his," using the feminine pronoun

41

exclusively for the first few paragraphs or pages, just as if I believed that all human beings are female. Then, when there is a kind of break in the subject matter, I switch to the exclusive "he," as if I thought that all humans are male. One must be careful not to give the impression that one is writing about human beings who are alternately male and female, or even worse, both male and female at the same time. Usually, however, a writer can avoid that kind of confusion with very little trouble.

I have been trying in this book to use this technique for balancing pronouns. The problem is further complicated, however, by the particular objectives of this work, namely to give the student-reader advice about how to write a philosophy paper. This purpose suggested a direct personal tone addressed to the reader and about her problems, just as if I were writing her a letter, in which I frequently refer to her experience and her problems. As a consequence I fell into the practice of using the second person singular pronoun, "you." So instead of sentences like "An architect should design her own house," there are typically sentences like "As an architect you will want to design your own house." The latter gives the writer no discretion to select the gender of a pronoun. On some pages in this book, there are ten or more times as many uses of "you" as of "he" or "she." Moreover, this book does not have long stretches where one form of gendered pronoun may be used exclusively without creating confusions over identity. At the beginning of Chapter 7, to take one example, I distinguish three offices: that of teacher (professor or her assistant), student, and textbook author (me). I selected the masculine pronoun to refer to the textbook-author because of the association with me. The professor in the course I made a woman. (Similarly at other places I made her assistant also a woman.) The student, to whom I imagined myself talking directly, I made a woman too. So of the three persons I make reference to two by means of the feminine pronoun and two by the masculine pronoun. If however, I had made all of these persons the same sex, there would be a danger of ambiguous reference. This possibility is not clearly illustrated by an imagined single sentence pulled out of the context that could provide clarity. But there are contexts in which the reference to the pronoun would be uncertain at the moment it is uttered. In *some* contexts at least the following words would be confusing:

✧ **She gave her book back to her.**

Who gave whose book to whom? If the author too were a woman, we would not even be clear whose book is being discussed. Examples of this sort show how useful grammatical gender can be.

(7) *Double negatives.* This category should be understood in the same way we understand the rules requiring agreement in number mentioned above.

✧ **He don't know nothing.**

✧ **She never gets nowhere.**

Double negatives in natural language, we concede, have nothing to do with logic. Some widely used natural languages (for instance Spanish) include double negation in their standard forms and this doesn't disqualify them for the study of logic. Double negation does fail the ear test, it is not sanctioned by usage, it is hardly ever used in serious formal prose (in this respect it is like "ain't" and "she don't care"), and (unlike "ain't") it is surpassingly ugly to the educated ear. If you use a double negative in a philosophy paper, you will slow down and confuse your professor—unless it is clear in the context that you have resorted to the vernacular for comic or sarcastic purposes.

(8) *Different from or different than?* This is an easy one, judging from the unanimity of the grammarians. The word "than" goes with relations between (or among) things in which one of the objects is quantitatively or qualitatively greater or better in comparison with the other. Merely being different is not a way of being greater or lesser, better or worse. When only a difference is being stated, one does not use the ranking term "than." One thing can be different *from* another without being greater (in any sense) *than* the other. This is another rule solidly based in educated usage that seems to be undergoing erosion. Nonetheless the support is still strong enough so that the following should be classified as an error:

✧ **Southern voters are different than northern voters.**

One of the reasons grammarians retain their confidence even in the face of eroded usage is that the mistaken usages embody a clearly recognizable confusion, easily extracted and explained.

(9) *Which or that?* This is sometimes a difficult option. Grammarians over a century ago decided that this distinction needed tidying up. They recommended a rule and gave arguments for its utility that were so subtle that they were very nearly philosophical. Grammarians apparently enjoy philosophical riddles, even artificially contrived ones. And that may be part of the incentive for preserving this difficult distinction. A new consensus apparently has formed in favor of jettisoning the old rule. The usual formulation of the rule now is very simple with subtle exceptions granted for "stylistic reasons" or for being "odd sounding." The current simple-sounding rule is as follows: When referring to an inanimate referent, that is, something whose gender is "neutral," use the relative pronoun *that*—not *which*—for restrictive clauses; use *which*—not *that*—for nonrestrictive clauses. The simplicity results from the transfer of complexity to a different source, namely the distinction between "restrictive" and "nonrestrictive" clauses. A clause introduced by a pronoun is called "restrictive" when it more narrowly restricts the reference of the term it qualifies by providing information that further defines it. A nonrestrictive clause, on the other hand, does not narrow the definition of the antecedent term so much as give further information which happens to apply to it. Thus,

• **Shoes that squeak are annoying to most people.**

is an example of a restrictive clause, and

43

- **Boots, which, unlike sandals, are likely to squeak, are not often worn by spies or burglars on housebreaking missions.**

contains an example of a nonrestrictive clause. The clause in the first example is restrictive and must be introduced by "that," whereas the clause in the second example is nonrestrictive and must be introduced by "which." The clearest examples of nonrestrictive clauses are those which add information *incidentally*, or at least *as if* incidentally, or to which the word "incidentally" could be added without distortion of meaning.

An easier test of whether a clause is restrictive or nonrestrictive is whether or not it is properly set off by commas. In fact, you are well advised to apply this test directly in deciding whether to use "that" or "which," and forget about the difficult distinctions between restrictive and nonrestrictive clauses. You might then decide between "which" and "that" in the following way. If it is part of a construction that can be separated by commas, use "which." If not, use "that."[9] Of course, the problem may still remain of explaining when commas may properly be used in this way, or deciding hard cases, but as a practical test and guide it is extremely helpful.

- **Respect for military values, which [incidentally] is found more frequently in the south, appealed to her.**

- **Leather shoes, which [incidentally] squeak more loudly on rainy days, are especially likely to have this disadvantage.**

- **Respect for military values that derives from family histories is more likely to be enduring.**

The following two examples violate the rules and are therefore ungrammatical:

- ◇ **Avowals which come from the heart are especially effective. ("which" should be replaced by "that")**

- ◇ **The stock exchange, that unfortunately is closed today, teaches us this lesson. ("that" should be replaced by "which")**

Almost all grammarians who defend this rule admit that there are numerous exceptions to it, and attribute the exceptions to "stylistic reasons." I would recommend departure from the rule whenever it sounds odd to the ear. Further, one should switch from "that" to "which" if the sentence is complex and already contains two or more "that"s. Thus,

- ◇ **Books that are bound in leather that is imported from that part of France that is closest to that part of Spain, are most likely to have the virtues that that sort of use requires. (It is infelicitous to have consecutive *that*'s, although not incorrect. It would be preferable to write "virtues *which that* sort of use . . .")**

---

[9] I owe this commonsense suggestion to Linda Radzik.

✧ **". . . that part of France that is closest to that part of Spain that ... (Change second "that" to "which".)**
In general it is more likely that a "that" can properly be changed to a "which" than vice-versa.

• **The cookies which I like best are chocolate.**

is acceptable.

• **The stock exchange that unfortunately is closed today.**

probably distorts the intended meaning, unless there should happen to be two stock exchanges in the speaker's city only one of which is open. Of course, a grammarian has no direct access to a writer's intentions, and whether her words are grammatical or not depends on what it is she wishes to say. Thus, "The argument, which comes [incidentally] from Plato, is mistaken" means something quite different from "The argument that comes from Plato is mistaken." A writer's failure to use the correct relative pronoun ("which" or "that") may have as its consequence that she says something that she does not mean. If the choice between "that" and "which" seems to be too difficult, as in the preceding sentence, one can decline to use either pronoun.

Another class of relative pronouns raises fewer problems. The pronoun "that" can refer, depending on the writer's meaning, to persons, animals, or things, but "which" can refer to animals and things, but not to persons; and "who" or "whom" to persons only. Thus we can refer to

• **. . . the man who came to dinner . . .**

or

• **. . . the man that came to dinner . . .**

but it is ungrammatical both by the ear test and the grammatical rule to refer to

✧ **. . . the man which came to dinner . . .**

In summary, the rules governing the distinction between "that" and "which" should be respected and observed when their violation might misrepresent the writer's own meaning, though it is perfectly permissible to depart from the rules where meaning is not likely to be distorted, or when the pronoun required by the rule sounds odd or stilted to the ear. That these exceptions are now so frequently encountered suggests that the rule is in the process of rapid erosion.

(10) *Prepositions as last words.* If style and readability are important to you, then a preposition is not a good thing with which to end a sentence. This judgment, however, is more like a recommendation of technique than a rule of grammar. As a grammatical rule it is indeed a good candidate for what Winston Churchill once

called "the sort of errant pedantry up with which I will not put."[10] The truth in the judgment is an instance of the more general principle that the "weightier" (more important or significant) words should be the ones that are given the greatest emphasis, and that this is more efficiently done if they occur at the end of a sentence. The best writers tell us that they are always prepared, especially in this period of labor-saving computers, to switch the locations of weightier words and phrases in a sentence to a more strategic place closer to the end. Prepositions are among the lightest words in the language and should not therefore be given the place of greatest importance. That is not to say that ending a sentence with a preposition is a "grammatical mistake," never to be done. It is a poor, inexpressive, ineffective use of language, but, for all of that, perfectly grammatical. (In my first draft the sentence preceding this one ended in "for all that." Now that it ends in "perfectly grammatical," the reader is more likely to get the point.)

In scholarly writing, there is another reason why it is almost always poor policy to end a sentence with a preposition. It can seem an inappropriately "breezy manner."[11] Moving the preposition forward need not always be "errant pedantry." It could have the desired effect of changing an informal style to a formal one, where that is called for by the circumstances. Similarly, ending a sentence with a preposition may be a way of changing stuffy and stilted formal prose to something that strikes the ear as more natural. Joseph Williams presents the following pairs of examples of this contextual variation:[12]

- **The peculiarities of legal English are often used as a stick to beat the official with.**

◇ **The peculiarities of legal English are often used as a stick with which to beat the official.**

and

◇ **The man I spoke with was not the man I had been referred to.**

- **The man with whom I spoke was not the man to whom I had been referred.**

Which sentence in each pair should we use? That depends on our purposes. If our situation seems to call for more formality, if for example we are writing a formal letter of complaint to some official or a scholarly book recalling some bit of history, then the formal mode might be more effective. But what is effective and what is correct are often two different things, and a

---

[10]This line has been attributed to Churchill by various writers, but there is no agreement about the historical occasion for the remark. See John Bartlett, *Familiar Quotations*, 16th edition (Boston: Little, Brown and Company, 1992).

[11]For a criticism of the "breezy manner" as a flaw in some journalistic prose, see Strunk and White, *op. cit.* (see note 6), pp. 66–67.

[12]Williams, op. cit. (see note 4), p. 187.

counsel of wisdom telling you "how to do it well" is quite different from a rule telling you what is permitted.

(11) *Split infinitives.* Here at last we have an example of a grammatical rule that is purely arbitrary, with nothing whatever to recommend it, except in rare cases for the most subtle of stylistic reasons. Educated people sometimes find it natural to split infinitives, and sometimes strangely and stubbornly to attempt to keep an infinitive unsplit. The rule then has no foundation in the usage of any relevant group of persons; it creates awkwardness rather than clarity; the original reasons once given in its support are long forgotten.

There is, however, at least one class of cases in which the rule forbidding split infinitives has a point. This class of cases can be labeled "Hopefully split infinitives." The adverb "hopefully" became popular during the presidency of John F. Kennedy, who used it frequently in reference to his own attitudes and actions, and a way of making qualified optimist predictions at press conferences. When a reporter would ask him whether he expected some particular happy issue from his problems, he frequently replied not "I hope so," but rather "Hopefully, that will happen," or "Hopefully, someone will do that." In this usage "hopefully" is not an adverb describing how the "somebody" would do the action Kennedy hoped for (namely, in a spirit of hopefulness). Rather, it is applied to the attitude of the speaker (Kennedy himself) toward its being done at all. It was as if Kennedy had made his optimistic prediction by saying "Hopefully speaking, that shall be done" where the adverb clearly refers back to the attitude of the speaker, and not to the hopeful expectations of someone else to whom the speaker is referring. Other adverbs have similar functions. There was a character in a Broadway stage play in the 1930s who, when asked his opinion of anything, would reply "Confidentially, it stinks."[13] The adverb here does not refer to the manner in which the other thing does its "stinking." It refers to the speaker's insistence that his own opinion be kept secret (confidential).

A "hopefully split infinitive" is one kind of split infinitive, at least, that ought to be forbidden by a rule of grammar. Perhaps it would be better to label it a "hopelessly split infinitive." A sports commentator on television recently said, for example,

✧ **The team will try to hopefully win the game.**

This statement is a clear but ungrammatical way of saying that the team will try to win, and the television commentator hopes they will succeed. But when he inserts the adverb between the split words of the infinitive "to" and "win," he implies that it is the hoping of the team he wants to talk about, not his own hopes, and that is simply not the case.

The clearest examples of unfortunately split infinitives, however, illustrates no such profound difficulty. They are still another set of errors of

---

[13] *The Man Who Came to Dinner.*

placement (see the first page of this chapter) directing the reader's attention away from the point the writer is trying to make. In a strangely self-defeating effort, the writer constructs a wall of words between the reader and the message the writer intends to communicate. I found a typical specimen of that mistake in a newspaper article:" No one likes the fact that 14-and 15-year-old girls are having babies ... yet we can't seem to, as a community, as a state, decide how we confront this."[14] Six words separate "seem to" and who it is that does the seeming and what appearance it is that these people have. The problem for the reader is not that the sentence is simply ambiguous, and therefore its message uncertain. The main problem is that contrasting words in the wrong place make it cluttered. An uninterested reader will come to the thoroughly smashed infinitive, go back to the beginning, and start over.

(12) *Who (or whoever) or whom (or whomever)?*   Many students find the standard directions for the use of this distinction to be one of the hardest grammatical rules to apply. Before we consider the hard cases, however, we should glance at the rule, which appears at first sight to be simplicity itself. "Who" acts as a subject of a verb; "whom" acts as the object of a verb. "Whom" also acts as the object of a preposition. In deciding whether to use "who" or "whom," look at the clause or phrase the pronoun will fit into, and consider whether it will be the subject or the object of that clause or phrase. It is correct to say:

- **Jones, who had defeated her opponent in two earlier elections, was confident.**

And it is correct to say:

- **Later that evening I met the woman whom everybody expected to win the prize.**

and

- **The man whom I saw in the car was the chief of police.**

Similarly, it is correct to say

- **During the intermission I met the man *who* had earlier eliminated me from the tournament.**

and also to say that

- **During the intermission I met the man *whom* I had earlier eliminated from the tournament.**

Both of the following, however, violate our simple rules, and have to be declared ungrammatical:

---

[14] "Lawmakers do little to lower teen pregnancy rate," *Arizona Daily Star,* Tucson, Arizona, March 24, 1996, p. 1.

✧ **I met the man** *who* **I had earlier eliminated.**

and

✧ **I met the man** *whom* **had earlier eliminated me.**

For many students the situation becomes uncomfortably complicated when the personal pronoun to be selected will be subject of its own clause but that whole clause will be (say) the object of an earlier preposition. Thus, in

• **Give it to** *whoever* **comes in the door next.**

who is subject within its own clause but that whole clause, in turn, is object of the preposition "to." In a case like this, it is not the prepositional phrase that is determinative, but rather *who comes in* (the verb clause), and the pronoun's role in that clause, that determines whether the subjective or objective pronoun is used. Thus, in

• **Give it to** *whomever* **you wish.**

the *whomever* is in the governing position, which here calls for the objective pronoun, and the following is a mistake:

✧ **Give it to** *whoever* **you wish.**

In general, grammarians mean by the term "clause" a group of words containing a subject and a predicate capable either of functioning independently, in which case it is itself a sentence, or of forming a part of a larger compound or complex sentence. Typically, English clauses contain a verb and other words whose function is best explained by their relation to the verb in their clause. Where there is a verb there will also be a *subject* of that verb, the person or thing that does the action indicated by that verb. "I think" identifies me as the doer of a deed (thinking)."The leaky boat sunk" identifies the boat as the subject of the "act" of sinking. Similarly, when some person or thing is acted upon by the subject in the manner indicated by the verb, then that person or thing is the *object* of the verb. So if you punch Jones, kiss Smith, address Brown, understand Green, recommend Johnson, then those people are all objects of your various actions, and if you write a book or cook a meal, the inanimate objects are affected by your action as indicated by the verbs "write" and "cook." At this point suppose we have good practical reason to substitute a pronoun for a noun in the clause from which the noun has been removed. Instead of saying "Joel kissed Betty" we say, for example, "He kissed her." Sometimes the pronoun plays its assigned role as a stand-in for a noun in this simple fashion. On other occasions the pronoun mediates the transfer of information that will help us identify what person or thing is to be represented in its clause and whether that thing will be related to the verb in the manner of subject or object. If the substitution is to be in the role of a subject, then one form (who, whoever) is used. If the entity is to be an object, then another form (whom, whomever) is used. If the thing referred to is an inanimate entity like a rock, say, then no form of who/whom is used, and instead we say "which" or "whichever."

In deciding whether to use "who" or "whom," a writer must look at the clause into which the personal pronoun is to fit. If the designated entity is to be the subject of the verb in that clause, then use "who." If it is to be the object of the verb then use "whom." Which of these pronoun forms is correct is determined by its function within the clause and *not* by the function of that clause in the larger sentence. As said above, a whole verbal clause with its own subject and predicate may function as object of an "external" preposition, for example the English word "to" or "for" or "by" or "under." Alternatively, the whole verbal clause may function as the object of some verb from elsewhere in the sentence, as in "He told (the 'outside verb') whosoever would listen." Normally when we see a preposition, we expect the word directly following it to be its object and therefore take an objective form. The same is true when we see a verb. But we can be too hasty. "I brought it for (the 'outside preposition') her" is not a good model for understanding "I brought it for whoever wants it." The word directly following the preposition here is not itself the object of the preposition "for." Rather, it is the final word in a prepositional phrase, which, as a whole phrase, functions as object of the preposition. So the pronoun in one simple sentence is an object in relation to its own verb, and part of a larger phrase that is the object of a preposition elsewhere in the sentence. And in cases like this it is the role within its own clause that is the determinative one.

But just when we think we have the rule mastered, some permissive liberal grammarian will point out that many superior writers frequently violate it for no better reason than that its violation in the circumstances pleases the ear or that many educated writers habitually violate the rules for similar reasons. We would be rejecting their writing as "grammatically mistaken," but even the most stubborn purist is forced to concede that such a judgment would be pedantic. Fowler gave many examples of uses of "who" and "whom" by distinguished jurists, parliamentarians, and critics, as well as the "colloquialisms" of ordinary folk, that fit this description: "Who did you hear that from?" and "The Queen asked her Prime Minister about who she should summon to head the government."[15] Oddly, there seem to be as many mistaken "whom"s as mistaken "who"s, despite Henry Shaw's confident assertion that "Because most people consider *whom* less natural than *who,* they sometimes disregard grammatical requirements and use *who* even when *whom* is clearly indicated."[16] Shaw even recommends to the confused beginner: "unless you are reasonably certain that *whom* is required, use *who.* You will be right more than half of the time."[17] The value of this

---

[15]Fowler and Gowers, *op. cit.* (see note 3), p. 708.

[16]Harry Shaw, *Dictionary of Problems: Words and Expressions* (New York: McGraw-Hill Book Company, 1975), p. 255.

[17]*Loc. cit.*

advice depends on how prone one is to the two types of mistake. On the other side of the controversy about relative pronouns, Fowler listed dozens of examples from respected journalists and historians,[18] examples of the form

✧ **Lord Montgomery liked to have around him only men *whom* he knew respected him.**

The clause that governs the writer's choice of pronouns here is "*who* respected him," and the role of the pronoun in that clause is subjective. This "mistake," using *who*, not *whom*, is now made so frequently that some of the purest grammarians have despaired over it. Fowler and Gowers call it one of "those *sturdy indefensibles* of which the fewer we have the better . . ."[19]

SUMMARY

The best advice to the beginning student is to conform to the "rules of grammar" as best you can. Otherwise you will seem illiterate, unpolished, uneducated, even vulgar; and that ain't good. It is also good advice not to conform to grammatical rules at the cost of sounding odd or pretentious.

The authority for any grammatical rule is usage that is worthy of respect. Where usage and the rule are in opposition the rule must already have become vestigial. It is interesting that grammar, in one of the meanings certified by *Webster's* ("a study of what is to be preferred and what avoided in the inflection and syntax of a language"), is a thoroughly normative enterprise. Some word usage is to be *preferred* and some *avoided;* some is good and some is poor; some effective some ineffective; and so on. But when we make *rules* our model, we can, in addition, speak of what is and what is not *permitted,* what is required and what is allowed, what is grammatical and what is not. These ruleconnected categories suggest legal-like language, as if the grammarian were a lawyer or a moralist. There is a difference, however, between grammatical permissibility and legal permissibility, which can be brought out by considering the question: "How binding is a rule of grammar?"

The fact that a legal rule is poorly designed, or likely to be inefficient or unfair in its assignment of burdens, is not a reason, or at least not a conclusive reason, for disobedience. We have a duty as citizens to obey the valid legal rules of our community on pain of punishment. But if a rule of grammar confuses language users, impedes communication, or makes conscientious speakers sound odd, we have strong and often decisive reason against conformity to the rule.

The rule of grammar in this case could remain binding only because a "frankly arbitrary" rule requiring right-side-of-the-road driving is binding, namely because it coordinates the activities of crowds of persons who would otherwise collide with one another (speaking literally as well as figuratively). There is no inherent

---

[18]Fowler and Gowers, op. cit. (see note 3), pp. 707–711.
[19]Fowler and Gowers, op. cit. (see note 3), p. 708.

superiority in a rule that mandates the right side rather than the left side for motorcar driving. The point is that we must have agreement in actual practice (compare "usage") if we are to pursue our separate ways harmoniously.

In this respect, rules of grammar are like the coordinating rules of the road. If we remained tolerantly silent as they are ignored, we would generate a kind of chaos in the realm of communication. Before English grammar was taken seriously in the seventeenth century, the written language even of educated English users already seemed a bit uncoordinated, if only from the lack of uniformity of spellings and punctuation. "For each person, his own spelling and punctuation rules" was not a slogan to render efficient written communications. On the other hand, to think of standard rules, uniformly followed, as leaving no room for exceptions, or to venerate such rules as if they were inherently rational for some reason deeper than the simple need for coordination, is to approach the line of errant pedantry.

If a rule of grammar has any rational force at all, it must be because it helps the writer and reader both, and promotes the cause of quick, efficient, and accurate communication between them.

What if everyone simply ignored grammatical rules, each following instead some speech patterns of her own design? Much would be lost. First, there would be a lot of repetitiveness, just as there is in spoken conversation when each party is difficult for the other to understand because of regional accent or speech defect. When a writer uses the word "whom" when "who" is called for, he may send his educated reader down the wrong track. In the railroad metaphor I have already used several times, the misused word or word pattern may be a pivotal switching point, and when the wrong pronoun is used she may find herself at a destination other than the one to which the writer meant to send her. In that case the reader will have to return to the switching point, learn what went wrong, and start over.

Closely related to the benefit to the reader when he is not slowed down in this way is the benefit to the writer who is confident that he is really saying what he means to say. It was once an oft-cited benefit of correct usage, that violation of a rule "put the wrong words in a speaker's mouth," as when he tells a physician that he "feels badly" when he means that "feels bad." That is, he says, without meaning it, that he uses the sense of touch poorly. Perhaps because of nerve damage he cannot distinguish cotton from wool by touching and rubbing the fabrics alone. They feel the same. *He* feels *badly*.

The example does not have the force it once had, however, because the ungrammatical sentence no longer strikes the ear as strange. By the ear test, it sounds quite natural these days to complain about one's health or to apologize for a hurt by saying "I feel badly." When grammatical people find themselves no longer in the majority, they might as well give up the struggle and write contrary to the no longer popular rule. In the end, people who want to be understood (and don't we all?) will violate the rule. And when *their* usage is shared by a large majority then the rule they violated can be said no longer to exist.

6

Some Common Mistakes in Diction

For the most part, grammatical mistakes consist in putting words (or groups of words) into relations with one another that subtly alter the way they function. Sometimes a group of words located at one place in the sentence would actually have a different meaning if it were moved to a different place in the sentence. The reader has seen examples in Chapter 4 of mistakes that consist in putting groups of words in the wrong order.

Errors of diction[1] are simpler than that. Our diction is defective when we select the wrong word for transmitting our meaning. The distinction between grammar and diction, so construed, roughly corresponds to a technical distinction in the theory of signs between *syntax,* which concerns the relation of words to one another, and *semantics,* which concerns the relations between words and what they refer to, when their primary function is to make reference. Some words, like "hurrah!" and "boo," "gosh," "gee," and "wow!," for example, do not function to make reference to things so much as to express, evince, or evoke feelings and attitudes. The word "cat," in contrast, makes reference to cats, small quadruped mammals that we all know how to recognize. If I write—

✧ **Meowing furiously, I picked up the cat.**

then I commit a kind of syntactical error, that of letting a participle dangle, thus affecting, at least momentarily, the meaning I intended to communicate. In contrast, if an immigrant whose English is weak uses the word "cat" to refer to what the rest of us call dogs, she has made a semantical error, that is, to say an error of diction. That she is in error is not merely an opinion of mine. It is a simple fact that the word "cat" refers to the creatures that meow, not to the creatures that bow-wow. If the immigrant stubbornly persists in her opinion to the contrary, then she is the one who is wrong. Her opinion is incorrect.

---

[1]The word "diction" is ambiguous. In the sense it bears in this book it has to do with word selection "with regard to correctness, clearness, or effectiveness" (Webster's 3rd Unabridged), but it also has a sense in which it concerns vocal expression primarily, enunciation in public speaking, and singing. The latter sense is not part of the subject matter of this book.

LINGUISTIC CORRECTNESS
AND CONTROVERSY

How can we be so confident that the woman who uses the word "cat" as we use the word "dog" is mistaken? Maybe the rule she violates is mistaken. Maybe all the rest of us are mistaken. Not very likely! It makes no sense to say that the semantic rule is mistaken. What could it be mistaken about? Perhaps it is in conflict with some higher principle of meaning. But then couldn't we raise the same skeptical doubts about the principle as we had about the rule? What would evidence be like that the word "cat" does not refer to the creatures we all refer to as dogs? The key to this mystery is in phrase "we all"—the virtual unanimity of English speakers. If every normal speaker interprets the word one way, and a single immigrant interprets it in another way, then by the only fact that can count as evidence, namely, the actual practice of persons in a given linguistic community, the word "cat" must refer to cats, not to dogs. But can there not be other types of evidence? Is there some authority whose decrees could support the "'cat' means 'dog'" position? Some people claim that the judgments of dictionary makers have this authority. Usually, however, when the so-called authorities do make a judgment of correctness or incorrectness, *they* themselves cite as evidence for their judgment no more than the fact of general usage.

The example about cats and dogs, however, creates a kind of artificial simplicity. Where there are actual controversies over the meaning of a word, the situation is always more complicated, and there really is some ground for the controversy. First of all, there is not always unanimity among normal speakers. Sometimes speakers will be divided nearly evenly. Sometimes they will disagree about the group whose usage is to be consulted, some restricting the qualified groups to experts. So, for example, there was a time when people disagreed over whether the word "fish" referred to whales and seals as well as to salmon and tuna. Most native speakers of English at that early time no doubt believed that the word "fish" does refer to whales. But a specially qualified group of experts (biologists) thought otherwise, and their usage prevailed in the end.

CONSTANTLY CHANGING USAGE

The most important factor in generating disagreements over the meaning of single words and phrases is the undeniable fact of linguistic change. Word meanings are in constant flux. In some cases the change is slow and steady, like much biological evolution. In other cases it is sudden and abrupt, almost revolutionary. One apparent consequence of constant change in word usage over the centuries is that what is—or what is thought to be—correct in one period becomes incorrect in another, and vice-versa. A given word-meaning may even go in and out of favor over the centuries.

A primary generator of change in word meanings is the undeniable fact that individual speakers in all languages tend to depart from what is considered "correct" usage. They have never been very impressed by an alleged duty to speak as their superiors require. These deviations then are condemned as *mistakes* according to the prevailing standards of the time, and it is considered bad form, and even irritating to others, to allow such mistakes to creep into one's personal manner of speech. But changes, "mistaken" or not, become models for other changes, as mistakes become models for more mistakes of the same kind. A given usage will be correct in one period, a simple mistake in the next period, and a source of confusion during the transition.

Native speakers throughout the world who ignore or neglect traditional usage persist in what purists call "errors." If the critics are too severe, ordinary folk will mock them as pedants and snobs, and cite the difficulty of communicating with educated people who are so far out of step with the "in-people" who set the current fashion.

LINGUISTIC LIBERALS AND CONSERVATIVES

Language theorists who take mistaken diction less seriously sometimes think of themselves as democratic spokesmen for the common folk. They tend to be permissive in their judgments of what is correct and incorrect. Sometimes they are called, by themselves or others, advocates of a "liberal" theory. Linguistic liberals are uncomfortable with the very idea of a "correct usage" about which some people, even a majority of people, can be "mistaken."

On the other side are the linguistic conservatives.[2] These are persons who feel threatened by change and wish to slow it down. They are troubled by the fact that the language of Shakespeare becomes more and more difficult for young English speakers to understand, and Chaucer seems to write in a foreign language. When language changes too rapidly, the links between generations in different historical periods weaken, and cultural treasures are lost in the process. For conservative linguists mistakes in language rankle. Why should mistakes become more acceptable, they wonder, as they become more widespread? As a correct usage becomes endangered, we should not just shrug our shoulders in resignation to the inevitable. Rather, they insist, we should struggle all the harder to enforce the traditional rules. The alternative is to suffer misunderstandings that defeat the very purpose of accurate communication.

---

[2]Linguists are conservative, when they are, only in the sense that they put great value on conserving forms of language that come to us from the past. There is no discernible correlation between this kind of "conservationism" and political conservatism.

In Chapter 4 we acknowledged that there are some grammatical rules which, like rules requiring motorists to drive on the right, have justification in terms of the need for coordination and the prevention of collisions. It is not that "everyone on the right" is inherently superior to "everyone on the left." The need is for everyone to be on the *same* side, not that they all be on the right side. Rather than being uniquely rational, the selection of the right side instead of the left was arbitrary. Much the same is true of grammatical rules. Their justification is to be found in their effectiveness in preventing misunderstandings and providing the assurance that we will all continue "to speak the same language." Rules of diction (semantics) typically have their justification only in facts about general usage. Explanations of what people mean by a given word is all that can be claimed for dictionary definitions which "lay down the law" about what words mean. When the definitions are correct it is because they are accurate descriptions of how people use language. For ordinary words, the definitions describe the verbal habits of ordinary people in this century, not necessarily in earlier times.

SAMPLE MISTAKES OF DICTION

The following are deviations from traditional academic word usage. If you use these words in the mistaken ways currently popular, then you use them at your own risk. The professor who grades your paper may be displeased, and grade you accordingly. To reproduce here the arguments, pro and con, for intolerance, will at least give you a sense of how such criticisms can be controversial, and what the general arguments of linguistic liberals and conservatives are.

(i) *"Criteria" for "criterion."* There is little reason to tolerate:

✧ **The criteria of materiality is whether an object is extended in space, according to Descartes.**

The word "criteria" is the plural of "criterion," so that the mistake here is a simple failure of agreement in number between plural subject and singular verb. The correct statement of what the writer intended is: "The criterion (singular) of materiality is (singular) extension . . ." Similarly, it is incorrect to make the corresponding mistake by using a singular form ("criterion") with a plural verb. Thus we can condemn:

✧ **The criterion of humanity are rationality and animality.**

A correct statement of this proposition is: "The criteria (plural) of humanity are (plural) rationality and animality."

It has been a surprising development in my experience as a grader of student papers that the word "criteria" is used incorrectly with ever greater frequency. Matching subjects and verbs in number would seem to be a simple matter indeed. Singular goes with singular; plural with plural. The problem, I think, is that many students do not recognize the plural forms of words that have a somewhat unusual pattern for generating plurals. Most English words stem from Anglo-Saxon, Latin, Scandinavian, and Norman French ancestors. "Criterion," however, is Greek, and Greek nouns ending in "ion" generate plurals typically by changing "ion" to "ia." (This point does not apply, however, to the dozens of English nouns that end in "tion" and are not of Greek origin, such words as "question," "station," and "creation.")

Using the plural "criteria" as if it were the singular form of this useful word (a criterion is a standard of inclusion, or identifying mark) is becoming a common mistake, if it is still a mistake at all. My expectation is that when the mistake becomes even commoner, perhaps in another fifty years, it will be pointless to resist it, and it will cease being a mistake. "Only time will tell," *Webster's* says, "whether it will reach the unquestioned acceptability of *agenda*," another Greek plural. The common English word "agenda," like "criteria" and "media," is a grammatically plural term widely used as if it were singular, as for example, "The agenda for the meeting is now ready." Technically, "are" should replace "is" or perhaps "agendum" should replace "agenda," but both of these changes would make the resultant sentences sound a bit odd to most readers. My advice to students is to continue to use "criteria" as the plural of "criterion," in the realization that the definitions of these terms are in flux. Perhaps rearguard defense against the new way is called for, but it will probably lose in the long run. In the meantime, the plural "criteria" still has the slight edge. Stay with it.

(ii) *"Disinterested" for "uninterested."* The struggle over the ordinary term "disinterested" is, from the conservative point of view, already lost. That is a shame, because there is an important and useful distinction between them. To be interested in something in this sense of "interested" is to be disposed to have one's attention or curiosity aroused by that thing, as for example when a person is interested in mathematics, or history, or baseball statistics. To lack such a disposition is to be uninterested in the subject. In a different sense of "interested," to be interested in some object is not merely to be intellectually absorbed in it, or to have one's attention likely to be absorbed in it, or to be curious about it; it is rather to have invested some part of one's own good ("interest," or "self-interest") in it. If I have an interest in (say) the General Motors Corporation, it is probably because I have invested money in the company so that what promotes *its* interest (well being or profit) also promotes mine. The antonym of this second sense, until recently, has been "disinterested," not "uninterested." The word "disinterested" has had a long and honorable career in law and political theory. Disinterestedness in this sense is genuine impartiality, which is the characteristic virtue of the judge. In a court of law we require that the judge be disinterested, that is that she not pursue her own personal profit at the expense of justice. On the other hand, we don't require her to be *uninterested* in the trial she is presiding over, in the way she is uninterested perhaps in non-Euclidean geometry or professional wrestling. We don't really care whether she is *uninterested*.

Here is some advice to the student: Do not use "disinterested" to mean "uninterested." The words are close enough together in meaning to cause confusion over what is meant, and distinct enough from each other to deserve separate words for the distinction. However, my impression is that the battle to preserve the distinction between "uninterested" and "disinterested," a worthy cause, is now virtually lost. We can feel sad about that, but we will, in time, be swept along.

One interesting irony is that I have written as if "disinterested" began its career meaning "impartial" and then decayed as a result of mistaken usage until it acquired (illegitimately) its present sense of "uninterested." Historically, however, that is a false account. "Uninterested" came first; then came the sense of "impartial," and now the pendulum is swinging back again to using "disinterested" as if it meant uninterested.

(iii) *"Enormity" for "enormousness."* It is easy to see how these two independently evolved terms have become confused. The similarity in their sound is striking and naturally leads one to expect a strong similarity in meaning. "Enormity," however, is a term of moral condemnation. It means "an outrageous, improper, vicious, or immoral act," "a great wickedness . . . monstrous, outrageous" as in "the enormity of the crimes committed during the Third Reich." The word "enormous" does not have this connection to immorality. It too refers to something immense, but the immensity it refers to is in physical size, as in—"The cave is enormous," "The planet Jupiter is enormous" etc. If we wish to make a noun to correspond to the adjective "enormous" with its exclusive concern with huge physical size, we should say "enormousness." "Enormity" doesn't do the job since it already carries the sense of "hugely wicked." One would not wish to refer to—

✧ . . . the enormity of the Grand Canyon.

Neither would one wish to refer to—

✧ . . . the enormousness of Adolf Hitler . . . (who was not very large)

If we end our discussion at this point, we will have overlooked the eroding effect of several centuries of misuse. It is no longer true of most English-speaking people, that they recognize "enormity" as referring to extreme wickedness, or that they have even heard of the word "enormousness." At least that recognition has been lacking in my students for a long time. Moreover, the word "enormousness" is long and ugly. My advice: use "enormity" if you wish, in both a moral and a physical sense, making sure that the context makes clear your intention. Again the argument from usage for the old way fails.

(iv) *"Fortuitously" for "fortunately."* Erosion seems only just begun on this one. It seems to me that only recently have people begun to say "fortuitously" when they mean simply "fortunately." Furthermore, the reason for the spread of the incorrect usage is that it sounds more impressive, one of the least appealing but most powerful motives behind incorrect diction. Since this error is relatively new, its spread through the population is only partial, and there is still time to resist it. A fortuitous event is one that happens not by design but by chance. That is the well-established sense, favored by critics and professors. A fortunate event is one whose results are welcome. Some fortunate events are fortuitous too, that is they occur by *lucky chance.* They are fortunate in that their luck was good luck. They are fortuitous because their good fortune was lucky (due to chance). The word "fortuitous" in traditional usage is perfectly correct if *it refers only to the element of chance.* It is not as strongly supported when *it combines chance with fortune* (as in "lucky chance"), though that is no longer thought to be objectionable. But the line is firmly drawn against using "fortuitous" simply for good fortune whether luckily produced or not.

(v) *"Infer" for "imply."* These are words prominent in the vocabulary of logic, and untypical uses of them will raise a logician's eyebrows and arouse his wrath. Even though they are not technical terms unfamiliar to the general public, their usage is correct only if it is firmly established in the usage, not of everyone, but of that segment of the educated public that "works in" logic. In a philosophy paper in particular, you don't want to say that—

✧ **'All dogs are mammals' infers that all puppies are mammals.**

Neither do you wish to say:

✧ **When Jones read Smith's message he didn't understand it at first, but by making certain assumptions he implied that it meant . . . so and so.**

The best simple formula for distinguishing these terms is that we *infer from* and we *imply to.* Only rational beings like humans infer, because inferring is a kind of mental or intellectual activity. To infer x from y is to draw a message from y that x is the case. On the other hand, sentences and propositions are not the sorts of entities that can infer. They have no minds or intellects. But they do imply to rational beings that certain propositions are true. To imply is to send a message out; to infer is to draw the message in. Any kind of fact can imply; only rational beings are capable of inferring. In the usage of logicians "p (proposition or statement) implies q" itself implies that a person who knows that p would be warranted to infer from it that q.

(vi) *"Refute" for "rebut."* This is an especially interesting case because it unites linguistic liberals and conservatives in agreement. The consensus is that it is always incorrect to use an achievement verb as if it were synonymous with a trial verb.

"He closed the door" is an example of a perfectly correct use of the achievement verb "to close," whereas—"Trying to close the door, she pushed it" is a perfectly correct use of the trial verb "to push." Other pairs of trial and achievement verbs are to attempt/to succeed, to swing at/to hit, to advise/to persuade, to impeach/to convict, to compete/to win, to implore/to convince. Sometimes the verbs come with their own preposition or adverb, and are best treated as contrasting single words in that form: to struggle against/to triumph over, to shoot at/to hit (or to shoot or to kill). It is not only a mistake to use an achievement word when what you mean is more accurately expressed by an attempt word, it is a serious mistake leading not only to miscommunication, but also to inappropriate action based on mistaken understanding. Using "refute" when what is meant is "rebut" is as clear an example as can be found of this confusion. If one candidate, Doe, gives a campaign speech in which he analyzes the state of the economy, and his opponent Roe argues back in disagreement the next day, it would be incompetent journalism for a newspaper to carry the headline: "Roe Refutes Doe." The wording would suggest that, in the opinion of the newspaper, Roe got the better of the debate, a very serious consequence indeed. This mere "mistake" in diction would function as an editorial opinion in a place reserved for purely disinterested fact-finding. What did happen, factually speaking, is that Roe expressed his disagreement with Doe in an effort to win the favorable regard of the voters. What the paper inadvertently said happened was that Roe succeeded in his effort, a "fact" that would have been clearly expressed by the achievement word "refute."

(vii) *"Irony" for "coincidence."* There is no more complicated word in the English language than "irony." A fully adequate account of its various meanings and their inter connections cannot be undertaken here. Suffice it to say that the adjective "ironic" is commonly applied to three types of subject: (1) expressions and actions, (2) impersonal events and states of affairs, and (3) attitudes. In the first category are uses of words to express something other than, and especially the opposite of, the literal meaning. In the third category (attitudes), "irony" is reserved for an attitude of detached awareness of incongruity. The second category, however, is the one in which the mistake of diction commonly occurs. It is correct to use the word "irony" for an occurrence with "the quality of being so unexpected or ill-timed that it appears to be deliberately perverse," as if impersonal nature could delight in frustrating us. The dictionary puts it thus: "A state of affairs or events which is the reverse of what was, or was to be, expected, as if in mockery of the appropriate result . . ."

The mere fact of coincidence is not sufficient to count as an irony in this sense, since a mere coincidence lacks the appearance of "deliberate perversity" and "mockery" essential to genuine irony. If Jones and Smith quite independently made plans to eat dinner at the Capriccio restaurant, then, when they encounter one another at that restaurant, that is a coincidence. Each may then say afterward that she met the other "coincidentally" at that restaurant. But the facts do not warrant the use of the word "ironically." Neither party was frustrated or harmed by the coincidence; neither did the circumstances appear as if "in mockery" of them. Therefore, it is a mistake of diction to say

❖ **Ironically, Smith chose to eat at the very same restaurant that Jones had selected for her dinner.**

A coincidence is ironical when, for example, what one person means to do to another is done to himself instead, and by the very mechanism he had intended to use to harm the other. Or when a congressman is convicted of violating the very rule he had himself drafted into law. This so-called "boomerang effect" is a clear striking example of irony. The most striking example of "as-if mockery" comes from the remarkable man who was among the first to explore the Grand Canyon:

> And there were stories current of parties wandering on the brink of the canyon, vainly endeavoring to reach the waters below, and perishing with thirst at last in sight of the river, which was roaring its mockery into their dying ears. To die of thirst while all around water thunders is as if to be taunted by fate as it destroys you. In this manner has the "irony of fate" often been conceived.[3]

The next time you are tempted to begin a sentence with the adverb "Ironically" simply because you are describing a coincidence, think twice about doing it. And manage to reserve one of those thoughts for the brave explorers who died from thirst in the monumental presence of millions of gallons of water.

---

[3]Powell, J.W. *The Exploration of the Colorado River and its Canyons* (New York: Dover Publications, 1961), p. 35, first published 1895.

7

Stylistic Infelicities

THE CONCEPT OF STYLE

Like grammatical and dictional "correctness," style is thought to be a feature of writing that is independent of content. In that sense, style is a *formal,* rather than a substantive, characteristic of written composition, a characteristic not of what is said but of how words are used to say it. Furthermore, like grammar and diction, style is subject to *evaluation* on independent grounds. A style can be praiseworthy even when what is said in that style is false, or the arguments in support of it are weak. And of course the opposite is also true. A style may be flawed even when used to make a strong argument with a true conclusion in grammatically correct language, and without the misuse of any individual words.

In another way, however, style is easily *contrasted* with grammar and diction. Despite its formalism and its liability to judgment and criticism, style is not governed to the same degree by rules. Style can be good or bad, pellucid or opaque, but not "correct" or "incorrect," any more than a sonnet in poetry or a sonata in music[1] can be judged "correct" or "incorrect." In virtue of their style, poetry and music can be beautiful, or plain, or ugly, but they are not indicted for rule violations. Indeed, nothing is more inimical to literary style than the application to it of rigid rules.

PROSE WRITING AS A SOURCE OF PLEASURE

The point of most papers or articles is to communicate some message to its audience. The closer the message received is to the one the writer intended to convey, the more effective the written communication is. Judged therefore against its purpose, an article is "well written" to the degree that the author's use of language does not create any artificial impediments to communication between the writer and her audience. In order to efficiently

---

[1] I mean by "music" the product of the *composer's* labors, a written score which can be thought of as the composer's directions to performers, who in turn produce music in the sense of what we listen to. It does make sense to say that the orchestra's performance or the conductor's interpretation was (say) "incorrect." But the composer's written directions can be neither "correct" nor "incorrect."

discharge its function then, a written article must possess the first virtue of composed essays: *clarity*. And in order to achieve clarity, an essay must possess some other virtues that are means to clarity. We can call these "the communicative excellences," and list among them such means to clarity as plainness, simplicity, unpretentiousness, brevity, balance, rhythm, and fluidity. Perhaps the word "readability" would do as well as "clarity" for the communicative virtues. A "readable" article is easy to read and difficult to misinterpret.

Good prose writing, however, need not be all business. In addition to transmitting messages, a written article may also try to communicate in such a manner as to cause pleasure or enjoyment as extra-communicative ends. We can call each of the excellences that make this enjoyment possible a "stylistic virtue," and contrast it with the communicative virtues which are means to clarity.[2] Excellences of style are those by means of which a prose essay produces enjoyment apart from whatever pleasure may come from the *content* of the communicated message. These include variety, balance, and cadence, which in turn are means to *flow* (a word I shall use in preference to "fluidity"). Flow is to the stylistic virtues what clarity is to the communicative ones. We can also distinguish the various subclasses of stylistic excellence. First there are the *poetic* ones borrowed for more prosaic purposes. These are the excellences that when restrained by, and coordinated with, communicative goals efficiently pursued, yield literary *elegance* or rhetorical *eloquence*. One thinks of Jefferson and Lincoln. Among philosophers, those who expressed their philosophies in poetic form include Lucretius,[3] Dante,[4] and Goethe.[5] The most eloquent of the twentieth-century philosophers was George Santayana.[6] Stylistic excellences in general provide a decoration to a communication, as gift wrapping does for gifts. *Adornment* is decoration of an elevated kind.

Our response to some classes of stylistic excellence is, whether we know it or not, our response to the character (in some cases) or the mood (in others) of the writer herself. We may describe an essay as "cheerful," "lively," or "urbane," or as

---

[2]Of course a given trait may be an excellence in both of these ways at once. An independent source of pleasure may be the way a passage "flows." At the same time, flow keeps the reader's attention directed and thus serves the end of communication.

[3]Lucretius. *On the Nature of Things*. trans. by Cyril Bailey (New York: Oxford University Press, 1947).

[4]Dante Alighieri. The Divine Comedy. trans. J.A. Carlyle and P.H. Wicksteed (New York: Modern Library, 1950).

[5]Goethe, Johann Wolfgang von. *Faust*. trans. David Luke (New York: Oxford University Press, 1987), Part One.

[6]George Santayana wrote many books and articles, but the excellences of his style at its best are as well shown in one small collection of essays as anywhere. I refer to his *Three Philosophical Poets* (Garden City, NJ: Doubleday, 1938).

"morbid," "flamboyant," or "peeved." These make a small sample of the hundreds of words in our language which evaluate, positively or negatively, character traits or more transitory moods of the moment. Such words may seem to include the literary characteristics of an article under consideration, but that use of them is secondary and derivative. We are really talking about the person who did the writing in question, and transferring our judgment to his style. It is not likely that we could separate style from character altogether, and concede that a given article is pompous, self-absorbed, or hypocritical, but nevertheless beautifully written in excellent style. Sometimes when you attribute a virtue or a failing to a person's style you are attributing traits whose primary application is to the writer himself. That is probably what F.L. Lucas meant when he wrote that "the foundation of style is character."[7]

THE PARAGRAPH

Chapter 6 on diction restricted itself to the consideration of single words or clusters of words, and Chapter 5 on grammar was limited to the study of sentences. The chapter on diction was confined to the "correctness" or "incorrectness" of word usage, while the chapter on grammar expanded its object of study to the interrelations of whole sentences. Remembering the practical purposes that distinguish a small manual like this one from a larger sort of textbook, we can say that this booklet is meant to help the student-writer select her words, and to teach her how to construct whole sentences out of them.

That description, however, does not exhaust this book's aims. This chapter takes on still larger units. The paragraph and more comprehensive parts like the section and the paper have their own structural complexity. Just as one can relocate words in order to restructure sentences, and move sentences in order to improve the style of the paragraphs of which they form a part, so one can move paragraphs to different locations in a section, and move sections to different places in a paper. In that way not only will the writer's own ideas be conveyed more accurately (that is, in a manner more closely corresponding to her intentions) but they will also be presented in the order that does them the most justice, keeping "secrets" until the most effective moment for revelation, setting surprises, and thereby drawing in the reader's interest in a way that will preempt her attention and keep her mind on the point without distraction or fatigue.

The mark of the paragraph is the indentation with which it begins. One can see at a glance that a line of inquiry or argument has, more or less, come to an end and another has just begun at the point of indentation. Indenting that first

---

[7]Lucas, F.L. *Style* (New York: Collier Books, 1962), p. 46, 47, *et passim.*

line is, therefore, a form of punctuation like a comma, a semicolon, or a period—an instrument for guiding the reader, ever so gently, to his starting and stopping places. Like these other conventional symbols of punctuation, but more visibly, the indented first line reveals at a glance when the next resting place will come, just as a sign on the highway enables drivers to estimate the time that must elapse before they have an opportunity to rest or eat.

Punctuation symbols, especially paragraph indentation, must be used deftly, according to some organizing principle, lest their appearance on the printed pages be random and functionless. One way of paragraphing would rely on the various independent steps of an argument to determine starting and stopping points. Another is to change paragraphs as one "changes the subject," which is to adopt another system that uses variations in meaning as the main guideposts for spacing.

Even if there were no very obvious spacing points as determined by the subject addressed or steps in a logical argument there would still be a practical need for punctuation and paragraphing. Herbert Read calls theories that emphasize certain nonrational grounds for punctuation "punctuation by respiration."[8] According to these theories, Read tells us, paragraphing and other punctuation are:

> determined by physical ease; it is assumed that what is read is really spoken, however unconsciously; and that since our natural speech is punctuated by the physical limits of respiration, our silent or imaginary speech should conform to similar laws. Each stop—comma, semi-colon, full-stop—represents a degree of pause.[9]

and evenly spaced pauses conform to the rhythms of the spoken language and regular patterns of inhaling and exhaling.

F.L. Lucas combines these two grounds for punctuation (logical steps and "respiration") adding that—

> At each paragraph-ending the reader can draw breath for an instant, and rest. The essential point is that he should also feel it a rational place to rest—that the paragraph in other words, should seem a unity. The considerate writer will not make such rests too rare. Short paragraphs make for ease and clarity. No doubt, if they are too short, the effect tends to become snippety, and the reader may feel he is treated as a half-wit.[10]

It is characteristic of aesthetic merit (and if Aristotle[11] was right, of ethical merit too) that one may fail to find the "just right" action, or "just right"

---

[8]Read, Herbert. *English Prose Style* (Boston: Beacon Press, 1955), p. 45.

[9]*Loc. cit.*

[10]Lucas, F.L. *op. cit.* (see note 7), p. 70.

[11]Aristotle, *Nicomachean Ethics.* trans. W.D. Ross (New York: Oxford University Press, 1925), Book Five, pp. 106–136.

language, or "just the right" musical note. Since the aesthetic objective is a kind of target, and a target can always be missed in at least two ways, by excess or by deficiency, by too much or too little, it follows that "just rightness" in art is likely to be a mean between two (or more) ways of missing. And so a paragraph can be too short or too long, and what is just right is the enemy of the excessive and the deficient. In Aristotle's terms, it is the "golden mean"[12] between extremes. Imagine, as an example of missing the target through excess, a whole printed page without a single indentation. While it is difficult sometimes for a writer to avoid so very long a paragraph, a unit of such dimensions will probably be too long. Its appearance is that of a solid block of print without gap or relief, and it can appear daunting to the reader.

My advice to the student paper-writer is to consider as an upper limit for the length of a paragraph, one full double-spaced page. If the paragraph begins half way down a typed page, say page 6, then it should not go further than half way down page 7. This cannot be a cut and dried rule. I intend it only as a rough rule of thumb subject to many exceptions. Similarly, I recommend that except in very special circumstances a paragraph should not have fewer than three or four sentences, assuming that the sentences in question are themselves of no more than standard length. If a paragraph has only a line or two, it will look like advertising copy, informal notes, letters, or the sort of unscholarly journalism associated with staccato shrillness. Lucas was not being oversensitive when he wrote that too brief paragraphs imply that the reader is a "half-wit."

There is no need, however, that each and every paragraph be roughly the same length, even if that length strikes the writer as the "golden mean." In respect to length, as to other things, the writer should alternate cadences, mood, and tone. Highly varied paragraphing converts written prose into something like conversation. It keeps changing its pace and its tone, but not at any cost. Try to preserve the isomorphism between stylistic alternation and the content of what is said in those various styles. One of the more common "infelicities of style" is *discursiveness*—a moving from topic to topic without order. A philosophical paper is discursive when it *rambles*. Discursiveness can often be interpreted as a flaw in the paragraphing techniques of a writer even when she determines paragraph boundaries by rational content (argument steps, change of subject, etc.). Careful consideration, typically at the stage of rewriting, must be devoted to paragraphing, else the paper will seem discursive. A reader knows when she is reading a discursive paper when she is inclined to ask at the start of every paragraph," What does this have to do with the subject under discussion at the end of the previous paragraph?" Chaotic as discursiveness can be when it jumps from one unrelated paragraph to another, it is even worse when the paragraphs ramble internally, jumping from one unrelated *sentence* to another.

---

[12]*Loc. cit.*

MOTION METAPHORS

Many metaphors are used to illustrate points already made, or to decorate poetically, or to cause a uniquely aesthetic sort of pleasure in the reader, quite independently of the reader's understanding or acceptance of the writer's thesis and argument. This interpretation, while often correct, however, is sometimes implausible. Especially when the subject matter of the article is philosophical, it is often practically impossible for either the writer or the reader to understand what is being said, except in terms of a kind of picture in one's mind, and with it a governing analogy. To illustrate this point about the unavoidability of metaphor, consider this and the following few paragraphs. These paragraphs are devoted to the presentation of a thesis about the role of metaphor, and in the course of explaining that thesis I shall assume it and apply it to itself.

The metaphor I shall be discussing appeals to the analogy of physical motion. Expository writing is bound in the imaginations of most of us with the idea of a voyage—a trip with a starting point and a destination, with byways and obstacles scattered along its route. The model of a good writing style is a smooth gliding progress through the water or across the ice. I imagine Olympic swimming races as presented on the television screen. The leader in the 400-meter butterfly stroke or the 200-meter breast stroke, or the sprint or medley relays, at their best, show hardly a ripple in the water, no choppiness, no splashiness, no wasted energies. Other images contributed by the Olympic Games are the rowing races, particularly the eight man shells. The boat, like the champion swimmers in the earlier example, may pick up a little current, so that its movement rate is faster, without losing its steadiness. A style that propels them at too fast a rate might interfere with their smoothness. As it is, the strokes come with a faultless regularity, that is at once conducive to efficiency and pleasing to behold for its own sake. The analogy here to writing papers is between physical grace and clarity (readability). Smoothness of flow, as we have seen, blends beauty and efficiency and is the ultimate stylistic virtue.

In explaining flow one must be careful not to give excessive emphasis to regularity of movement. The Olympic swimmer is not a well-oiled industrial machine. Neither is her performance valued as an antidote to insomnia, as would a set of random images of sheep jumping over hurdles. The flow that is the mark of superior style must also include variety, diversity, and alternation, and also something analogous to balance and rhythm.

The motion metaphors provide still other examples of how style can fail. If all of the passengers and crew of a small oceangoing ship were to move simultaneously to one side of the ship, perhaps to see some passing whales, the ship would tilt precariously. Its recovery, if it makes one, will be awkward and graceless, but if it does not recover its initial stability, it will tip over, destroying any semblance of the analogy to good style. Something like that debacle happens when one's prose is overbalanced on one side, and alternative meters and rhythms are neglected. The basic category here for the study of style is *variety,* and imbalance is just one particular way in which the virtue of variety can be absent.

Variety requires that some sentences be short and others long, and the same variation is helpful among paragraphs. Some sentences should be simple declarative ones with simple subject, predicate, and verb. Others, mixed in with them, might have three major independent clauses, each divided into a series of subordinate clauses in a spider's web of complexity. If there are too many of the brief simple sentences, the emergent style may be choppy or jerky. If there are too many of the byzantine-arachnid sort, then the dizzy reader will be lost in a maze. Still, in special cases, whole paragraphs may be composed of the one extreme type of sentence predominantly, if that is necessary in order to confer balance on the collection of paragraphs itself.

The biggest danger for beginning writers at the level of sentences is the possibility of their falling into a hurky-jerky rhythm. Herbert Read reminds us of this perilous path by putting the movement metaphor to good use again. "Such a sentence," he says, "betrays itself, if by nothing else, by its rhythm; it jerks along like a car in distress."[13]

It is an interesting fact that it is the long complex sentences and their counterparts among paragraphs that pose the greatest hazard for inexperienced writers who are aiming at stylistic virtues. Read cites[14] an uncharacteristic passage from Jonathan Swift: a single sentence of 110 words with subordinate clauses winding off in different directions like a network of branches in a bushy tree (no motion metaphor here!). The main pattern in the offending sentence resembles roughly the following caricature:

◇ **I spoke with *A* who agreed with *B*, an untrustworthy scoundrel, if I may judge by his affairs with *C*, although that was no worse, surely, than what *C* did to *B* who wrote about it to me later in his usual florid style, when I was basking in the warm Italian sun in the very vineyards that produce the best Chianti in Tuscany.**

This long (64-word) sentence is of course a gross caricature of the one Read finds in Swift. But like the original, it alternates incidental asides with subordinate clauses to produce a sentence that seems likely never to end. Read points out that in the original sentence "We . . . often come to a point which completes the sense of a possible sentence within the sentence. There is no suspense from beginning to end, but only an inorganic aggregation of phrases."[15]

---

[13]Read, *op. cit.* (see note 8), p. 44.

[14]*Loc. cit.*

[15]Read, *op. cit.* (see note 8), pp. 44–45.

Variety is so important an element of style that it should not be restricted narrowly to technical or measurable dimensions like length, number of words, and so on. Lucas is convincing when he writes—

Variety, indeed, in a wider sense—variety in mood, feelings, and tone— seems both a necessity for the writer and a courtesy to the reader. No one would entertain a guest on the same dishes for days; and no nervous system can go on responding without fatigue to one sort of stimulus, any more than an electric bell can stand being rung for hours ... a man of one mood or one manner tends to be as boring as a man of one book, or of one idea. Many-sidedness, both in life and literature, seems to me one of the great qualities . . .[16]

Obviously a writer who will frequently devote one hundred words or more, in one spin-off clause after another, cares little about gracefulness and flow. For whatever she gains by such excesses her reader will pay the price in monotony and gracelessness. Unrelieved pulsations cause a herky-jerky movement, little more comfortable than the back seat passenger's experience in a lurching trip down a bumpy road. No matter how good the writer's style is in other ways, she will weary the reader with it if it is unrelieved. George Santayana wrote some of the most beautiful sentences in our language, intricately patterned, their words "just right" and subtly interrelated, his metaphors fresh and colorful; but many critics have faulted his paragraphs for their lack of relief. In his earlier writings at least, Santayana's graceful sentences accumulate within paragraphs that are uniformly long and complex, without a place to breathe. His sentences, in other words, are not in balance. They cannot flow. As Herbert Read remarks

. . . the individual sentences may be rhythmical enough, but they do not form part of a more sustained rhythm; they follow in a series of minute percussions; they are like stepping-stones that finally weary the strained attention of the reader.[17]

A style of unrelieved staccato regularity, deficient in balance, without contrast in variation, will be deficient in balance, and as "moving" as a drum solo by a particularly ill-equipped and unimaginative drummer. Rhythm is important, but certainly not sufficient.

SMOOTHING THE FLOW

Fortunately, our language provides an abundant vocabulary and many literary devices for achieving variety, balance, rhythm, and grace. One can avoid the short choppy effects of unrelieved sentence and paragraph construction by

---

[16]Lucas, *op. cit.* (see note 7), p. 103.
[17]*Loc. cit.*

repeated variation of ways of beginning sentences. There are, for example, the parts of speech called conjunctions, and other phrases that function to smooth transitions. If one's sentences all have the bare minimum structure—subject, verb, predicate—then a linked sequence of them will have a jerky cadence:

Subject-verb-predicate.
Subject-verb-predicate.
Subject-verb-predicate.
Subject-verb-predicate.
Subject-verb-predicate.
Subject-verb-predicate.
Subject-verb-predicate.
Etc.

At this point the reader will be more than ready for some variation, and he can use many different literary devices to produce it. Consider—

Subject-verb-predicate.
And subject-verb-predicate.
For example, subject-verb-predicate.
But, subject-verb-predicate.
Therefore, subject-verb-predicate.
Moreover, subject-verb-predicate.
To be sure, subject-verb-predicate.
On the other hand, subject-verb-predicate. (But remember no reader has more than two hands.)
Fortunately, subject-verb-predicate.
Incidentally, subject-verb-predicate.
Ironically, subject-verb-predicate.
In any case, subject-verb-predicate.
In any event, subject-verb-predicate.
Alas, subject-verb-predicate.
Consequently, subject-verb-predicate.
Because the first subject-verb-predicate, **the second** subject-verb-predicate.
And endless combinations.

In addition to these vocabulary additives there are some familiar literary devices of similar function. The "ablative absolute" is a construction that can begin a sentence economically with a sweeping summary of what has gone on before: "Having finished his major work, Fitzgerald traveled to France for a holiday." "Caesar, having conquered Gaul, armed his troops for their return to Rome."

CONSPICUOUS OVER-USE
OF FAVORITE WORDS

Chances are good that if you submit a manuscript to the copy-editor at a publishing house, one of the most commonly made mistakes that she will discover and correct consists not in selecting the wrong word for what you want to say, but selecting the right word (the same word) too often. Readers get tired of overworked words. That may not be surprising in the case of technical terms (say in philosophy), but the typical terms selected for this kind of abuse are familiar ones in most people's vocabularies. Typically, the words are unusual enough to attract the eye and stimulate the memory. (Haven't I seen that eye-catching word somewhere? Recently? Two lines back? Oh.) Your teacher will suggest that you find a near synonym with which you can replace the offensively redundant term in its second or third or fourth appearance in a stretch only two or three lines long. The following example of such redundancy is from a recent leader among analytic philosophers:

✧ **When a person has no choice about whether a proposition . . . obtains . . . He cannot prevent that proposition from obtaining and so if it is unavoidable (relative to him) that it obtains . . . [then] he is not free to prevent it from obtaining.**

Forms of the verb "to obtain" are here used, in a way that is no longer widely familiar, four times. More than 10% of the words in the long quotation are "obtain" or one of its grammatical forms.

On second reading, the author should substitute words to replace "obtains" at the point where it interrupts flow and gets on readers' nerves, if the replacement terms are close enough to the writer's intended meaning to do justice to it. I advise the student-writer to keep for her own future use a list of near-synonyms for this purpose. In particular the list would include words from the philosophical vocabulary that proved exceptionally useful in the past. I can start a few such lists for now:

A. **The word "idea"** in the sense in which an "idea" of something is neither true nor false: "idea," "concept," "thought," "conception," "notion."

B. **The word "proposition"** (the meaning of a declarative sentence, that which **can** be true or false in what is expressed in language, that which is believed to be the case): Statement, contention, claim, affirmation, denial, assertion, proposal, thesis, theory, hypothesis, principles, opinions, convictions, beliefs, doctrines, declarations, holdings ("He held that . . ."), guesses, hunches, gut feelings. All of the above are nominative forms. Corresponding to most of them is a useful verb: To state that . . . , to contend that ..., he asserted that ..., she affirmed that . . . , my theory was that . . .

C. **Logical connection:** therefore, in which case, it follows that, consequently, because x is the case ..., since x then y, x is implied by ..., x is entailed by . . . , is **proved** by . . . , thus, hence, whence, wherefore, is supported by evidence.

D. **Qualification words:** however, nonetheless, nevertheless, but, on the other hand, in contrast . . .

E. **Supplementation words:** moreover, in addition, not to mention . . .

F. **Criterion:** standard, principle, **index**, test of, sign of, symptom of, typical of, paradigm of, paradigm case of, the very model of, prototype of . . .

G. **Purpose:** aim of, goal of, **purpose** of, the point of, the *raison d'etre* of, desire for, want, need . . .

Why compile a list only of *near* synonyms? There may be few exact synonyms in the language, and none of them may happen to coincide with the term you had vaguely in mind. But some of them may be constituent parts of larger constructions that are close enough in meaning to the word you wish to replace. The thesaurus uses a definitional shotgun, not a sharpshooter rifle. One of its pellets may actually hit the bull's eye if the aim was merely to splatter the target area. A writer seeking a word to substitute for "belief " simply for stylistic reasons may find that "conviction," while not exactly equivalent in meaning to "belief," is even better for conveying what the writer meant to say. Hence, it can be useful to have even near misses on your list.

FORGET ADORNMENT AND ELOQUENCE

There are no formulas, rules, principles, or instructions—not even "tips" about how to be eloquent. Eloquent writers in the past have testified that they do their most inspiring writing when they feel as if they have been taken over by a creative genius, not strictly identical to their everyday selves. Others mention intuition or spontaneous creativity. But since there is no reliable way of controlling these mystical states, and because the arguments of philosophy are themselves difficult enough, there is no point in aiming at literary adornment at the same time you master logical cogency, and the like. In nine cases out of ten the effort will backfire, and the resultant words will seem trite or silly.

Nevertheless, if achieving genuine adornment is important to you, there are safer methods available to you. The most reliable safe technique is imitation. Find a writer, preferably but not necessarily a philosophical writer, whom you admire, and copy word for word passages on blank sheets of

73

paper. Then shred the paper. There is a good chance that her characteristic rhythms will leave their mark on yours, that you will penetrate her technique for generating metaphors, or for modulating flow. After that, write your philosophy papers by thinking hard about a *philosophical* problem, and forgetting adornment and eloquence altogether. Don't be too hard on yourself. If you are an undergraduate student now, you probably have a half century still to acquire the literary knack. That should be enough.

One further caution: If it is the power of eloquence you seek, then begin by seeking it one sentence at a time. But if every sentence is eloquent your paragraphs will be crowded, jerky, and unreadable. It is not likely that you can become a brilliant epigrammist either, but it is a somewhat more realistic ambition. Finish your paragraph, preferably your final paragraph, and then having done your best to do the philosophical job, add one final sentence that sums it all up eloquently. Good luck!

TYPES OF POOR WRITING STYLES

As many as a few hundred words are commonly used to criticize writing styles, and several dozen of these fall into separate basic categories depending on the nature of the flaw they represent. First there are flaws that interfere with communication. Basically these are all forms of unclarity, curable by technical improvements that are possible, within limits, to codify. The names of some of these are metaphorical, for the most part dead metaphors—"opaque," "dense," "wooden," "wooly." Others describe a kind of uncomfortably restless feeling the prose style in question is said naturally to evoke in any reasonably sensitive person. The style is boring, tedious, or monotonous. Third, there is a group of terms that are specific in their description of the negative impact. They too can be opaque or boring, but their name specifies why it is that they have these unfortunate effects. These are words for aesthetic failures, language meant to cause pleasure as well as transmit information, perhaps even primarily meant to have that result, but which instead cause either a displeasure or no kind of feeling whatever, except maybe annoyance. In this category are language uses that are herky-jerky, out of balance, baroquely ornate, inappropriately and ineffectively poetic, colorless, too rapidly paced, or too slowly developing, and for some discernible reason or another, graceless.

In a fourth category are the human weaknesses applied to writing styles in a derivative way. Sometimes writing style reflects personal style. So when we disparage this kind of writing flaw, we are making a moral judgment about the character or personal manner of the writer. This is the most numerous class, and it includes "cute," "arch," "pompous," "pretentious," "sententious," "selfrighteous," "sentimental," "impersonal and aloof," "prideful," "coarse," "crude," "peevish," "cross," "vituperative," and many other flaws of both person and style.

Fifth, there are traits that belong to the writer, as far as we can tell, only at the time of her writing. Perhaps she was in a state too ephemeral to be called a character trait. It might nevertheless be a nasty or ugly state, a kind of dark mood that can come over almost anyone. So when a critic complains about the writing style that expresses this mood, he is really condemning the mood rather than the person, and his criticism falls short of moral judgment. Thus, we may complain about the style in which an essay is written by calling at an excessively "angry" or "gloomy" or simply "moody" style. We are especially likely to speak that way when the moodiness is to some degree independent of the content that is meant to be communicated.

Finally, sixth, what is objectionable in the style may be simply its *tone,* whether it expresses any particular mood or emotion. Writers do often have their own distinct tones—cynical, gushy, excited, sour, florid. A writer whose tone is promptly recognizable, and unpleasant, in one of these ways, may preserve her tone unchanged even when her mood is bright and her tone inappropriately dark (or so we might think), or when the content of her article is an opinion not normally associated with a tone of that sort.

In summary, whatever your writing is like, if it is not (1) opaque, wooden or wooly, (2) boring or monotonous, (3) graceless, (4) arch or cute (as an expression of a durable trait of character or personality), (5) uncharacteristically gloomy in mood, or (6) angry or cynical in tone, then there may still be hope for you as a writing stylist.

8

Language and Logic

The previous few chapters have been concerned with the clarity and presentation of one's ideas in written form. The next few concern the underlying logical reasoning of a good philosophy paper.

The task of philosophical writing is to persuade through the use of reason. Though a paper might be persuasive because it is rhetorically compelling, it will be unsuccessful as a piece of philosophy unless it makes a well-reasoned argument.

CORRECT AND INCORRECT REASONING

Logic is the intellectual discipline that distinguishes correct from incorrect reasoning. Reference to "correctness" will remind some readers of the concept of grammar. Another similarity in the two disciplines, logic and grammar, is that each goes well with the idea of *rules*. We speak of conforming to or violating the established rules of grammar, or, as the case may be, the rules of logic. And grammarians as well as logicians will defend their rules by citing the advantages of following them. Grammatical rules promote communicative efficiency and accuracy among their other benefits, and rules of logic can lead us quite infallibly from our true beliefs to other beliefs that cannot help but be true themselves. An important difference is that the logician has no choice but to accept the "correct rules" of logic. No logical rules change with a "consensus of logical usage." No logical rules are "useful but arbitrary" in the manner of traffic rules requiring drivers to stay on the right side of the road. Correct rules of logic are indeed useful. It staggers the imagination to picture a world in which they have no authority. But their utility derives from their correctness, not the other way round. They are as clear models of *objective* truth, or objective "correctness," as any that we have.

DEDUCTIVE AND INDUCTIVE REASONING

As we shall soon see, the direct concern of logic with "correct reasoning" is more precisely a concern with good and bad *arguments*. All arguments fall into one or the other of two basic types: deductive and inductive. There are several equivalent ways of defining "deductive." Deductive arguments claim not merely to give support, but to give *conclusive* or *decisive* support to their conclusion. They claim to *prove* or *demonstrate* that their conclusion is true, that its truth *necessarily follows* from its premises so that, if the premises are true (a matter to be investigated independently), then the conclusion *must be true*. It is *not possible* that it have a logically correct form where its premises are true and its conclusion false.

A deductive argument may have any number of premises, but we shall follow pedagogical custom, and adopt as our model of a standard deductive argument, one that has two premises and a conclusion. When we say of a given argument that its premises are false, we shall mean simply that *at least one* of its premises is false. (The issue will not arise in our brief discussion of inductive arguments.)

An inductive argument, as that term is frequently used by logicians, is best defined simply as a genuine argument that is not deductive. The terms "valid" and "invalid" are normally applied to deductive arguments only. Inductive arguments are subject to different terms of evaluation, good-bad, strong-weak, and so on. Unlike the terms of inductive evaluation ("highly probable," "moderately probable," "improbable," etc.), the terms of deductive evaluation, "valid" and "invalid," are not subject to degrees. A deductive argument is either wholly, unqualifiedly valid, or not valid at all. It cannot be just "a little bit invalid." Neither can it be the case that one argument can be more or less valid than another.

An inductive argument, then, is an argument whose conclusion is claimed to follow from its premises, not with necessity, but only with probability. One conclusion may be rendered more probable than another, and therefore be a better or stronger inductive argument. For example,

> Fifty children in neighborhood N regularly drank tap water from well G. Well G had 100 units of carcinogenic substance C per liter of its water. Only one child in neighborhood N failed to come down with leukemia during this period. The other 49 died of leukemia. In another neighborhood, where the well contained only tiny amounts of toxicity, there was only one case of leukemia. It is probable, therefore, that it was the presence of pollutant C in the drinking water from well G that caused the death of the 49 children. On the basis of these data, one cannot be certain of the conclusion, but this inductive argument shows it to be probable.

This inductive argument has several steps and thus is somewhat complex. The more simple and usual example of an inductive argument is that type called "induction by simple enumeration," in which a conclusion about all the members of a class is drawn from premises about some observed members of the class, which are fewer than 100%. If I examine huge barrels of nuts just off the tree at a nut orchard where there are several types of nut tree, I may take from the barrel a moderate sample of nuts in a dipper designed for that purpose. If, in examining the contents of my dipper, I find that it contains 12 walnuts, 4 pecans, and 1 almond, the discovery might tempt me to infer that most of the nuts in the barrel are probably walnuts. Indeed, the larger the percentage of walnuts in the sample, the higher the probability of that conclusion. The argument as it stands may derive support from an insufficient sample, or an unrepresentative sample, and there may be many other types of facts that could undermine the conclusion. So induction by simple enumeration may lead to more complicated problems for inductive reasoning than the simple inference with which it begins. Finally, I should mention here what is probably the most interesting form of inductive argument to philosophers, arguments from analogy, discussed below in Chapter 10.

SENTENCES AND PROPOSITIONS

Let us take a small detour at this point into the philosophy of language. Our purpose is to gain a better understanding of the basic components of logical arguments.

A *sentence* contains sounds (when spoken) or visible marks (when read) which in virtue of linguistic rules and conventions are taken to express beliefs, attitudes, or other mental states of the speaker (or writer). Some uses of language fall outside this over-simple classification—requests, commands, verbal performances like "I do" in a wedding ceremony, etc. But our exclusive concern here will be with statements of fact as typically expressed in declarative sentences. A declarative sentence is one that expresses the speaker's (or writer's) declaration that something is the case.

A *proposition* is what is asserted when a person utters a sentence, assertion, claim, etc. It is sometimes defined as the meaning of a declarative sentence. It has also been defined as that which can be true or false in a person's assertion. It should be noted that different sentences can express the same proposition, that is have the same meaning. Thus, "*La pluma de mi tia es verde*" and "My aunt's pen is green" both say the same thing. They are different sentences but they state the same proposition. They both have the same meaning. They both have the same truth value, that is, if one is true then the other must be true also, and if one is false, the other must be false as well. Even in one and the same language, two or more sentences may express the same proposition. "The pen of my aunt is green," for example, is a different sentence from "My aunt's pen is green." One contains seven words and the other only five. But they assert exactly the same proposition. Traditional logic has been concerned with whatever it is that is true or false. The best name for that entity probably is "proposition." (It is customary to use the letters "p," "q," "r," and "s" as abbreviations for propositions in symbolic representations of arguments that are made originally in ordinary language.) Logic is about propositions, not sentences.

ARGUMENTS

A set of propositions, one of which (the conclusion) is said to be true on the basis of the others (the premises). The conclusion is often signaled in ordinary English by the term "therefore." In logic, the traditional symbol for "therefore" is a triangle of dots, ∴. Thus the form of an argument is: "p, ∴ q," where "p" stands for one or more premises, and "q" stands for a conclusion. There are, however, many different ways of indicating which proposition is the conclusion. "It follows from p that q," "p consequently q," "because p is true, q is true," "the reason for q is p." Premises are often said to be *reasons* or *evidence* for their conclusions or to support, imply, entail, or require their conclusion. The nature of that support is precisely what the discipline of logic studies.

PREMISES AS UNPROVED ASSUMPTIONS

Ideally, we would do all of our reasoning in arguments that proceed to their conclusions from premises that are so obviously true that they need no argument in their behalf. Alternatively, we can imagine an argument, p ∴ q, in which p is not only a premise relative to the conclusion q, but a conclusion relative to further premises r and s. But what good does it do us to know that our conclusion follows validly from some premises if we have no argument to show that these further premises are true? There are at least four replies to this skeptical challenge, all of which are to some degree problematic: (1) The premises in our original argument are so obviously true that they need no further argument; (2) the premises in our original argument can themselves be proved (or at least rationally supported) in another argument employing a new set of premises, which in turn can be derived from still further premises, etc.; (3) the premises of our original argument must be recognized candidly for what they are, mere assumptions not capable of support by further argument; (4) an alternative argument can be given for our original conclusion, but it will be an argument in which that conclusion appears among the premises of its own proof (the conclusion in this case is assumed as a part of its own proof).

All of these replies directed at the skeptic have their own problems: (1) Propositions that have been debated for centuries among the wisest philosophers our civilization has produced could hardly be derived from premises so "obviously true" that they need no rational support themselves. (2) The second reply stares at a possibly infinite sequence of premises needing support, and if one proposition cannot be proved until an infinite collection of other propositions are proved, it would seem that the first proposition cannot be proved at all. (3) The third is the most reasonable reply, namely to develop a theory of knowledge that distinguishes among propositions on the basis of how reasonable it is to "assume" their truth, given that it is impossible to do so without undefended "assumptions" altogether. (4) To use a proposition as a premise in its own proof is certainly a flawed way of reasoning. Whether we go further and identify that flaw as "invalidity" in the technical sense need not be decided here. But "circularity" (as it is sometimes called, and "begging the question," which is still another name for it) is frequently committed in ordinary discourse, and theoretically is one of the most interesting types of flawed argument.

LOGICAL NECESSITY VERSUS PSYCHOLOGICAL CERTAINTY

A person may stand in any number of possible relations to a proposition. She can be absolutely confident that p is true, having no trace of doubt, reasonable or not. She may believe p with considerable confidence, but be prepared to recognize counter-evidence when she sees it, and to modulate her degree of confidence in its truth accordingly. She may have moderate confidence in its truth. She may have doubts that it is true. She may be certain that it is false. All of these degrees of certainty are defined as states of mind. If Dorothy is certain that p, a proposition about the cause of earthquakes, is true, that is a psychological fact about *her,* not a geological fact about the earth.

It is easy to confuse this psychological certainty with logical necessity. An argument of the form "If p then q; p; therefore q" is valid quite independently of any belief or any degree of certainty in belief any person might have toward it. That means that, given the truth of its premises, its conclusion must be true. Even individual propositions, as we shall see below, are sometimes necessarily true (when they are "analytic," or tautologies, or "true by definition," they cannot be false, though as we shall see they can be trivial). Similarly, propositions that have the form of logical contradictions *must* be false; they cannot be true. It cannot be true even of an infinitely powerful deity that He can both exist and not exist at the same time. To assert a logical contradiction is to say something of the form "p and not p," and all statements of that form are necessarily false. A rational person may believe p and another rational person might believe not p. But no rational person could believe both p and not p. In fact, no rational person could disbelieve "p and not p" with anything less than absolute psychological certainty. Rational persons match their psychological certainty to logical necessity, but those two conditions are not the same thing.

NECESSITY AND CONTINGENCY

Logical necessity can be attributed either to valid deductive arguments or to the truth or falsity of particular propositions. A valid deductive argument, as we have seen, is an argument that is such that *if* its premises are true, then in virtue of its form alone, its conclusion must be true. Some individual propositions are logically true or false. For example, "A is A" is logically true (though uninteresting) and "Some A is not A" is logically false. Their truth or falsehood, therefore, is in a sense "logical." Other propositions can be called "factually true." There is nothing on their face that signals their necessity. As the label "factually true" implies, their truth or falsehood is *contingent*. It depends on what the facts happen to be at the time it is asserted. It is factually true that whales are warm-blooded mammals. Whereas it is logically true, most philosophers believe, that if there are three balls in a jar, and I open the jar and add three more balls, allowing none of the balls already there to escape, and no new balls to enter, then there are six balls in the jar.

Traditionally, philosophers have made the distinction under discussion in the terminology of "analytic" and "synthetic" statements. By "analytic statement" they meant "tautology," a proposition whose truth is necessary. For most clear examples of an analytic statement, the necessity of their truth follows from the definitions of the words that occur in them. "All kittens are young cats" is true not because of some empirical fact that we discover by looking at the world, and we don't have to look over and over again to confirm our judgment of truth. That is to say, in the traditional terminology, that the status of necessary truths is *a priori* (knowable independently of experience). A synthetic statement is true or false depending on the facts and is knowable through experience or *a posteriori*.

THREE TYPES OF IMPOSSIBILITY

It is impossible for a being to exist and not exist at the same time, or in general for a being to have a characteristic and not to have that characteristic at the same time in the same part of itself. A self-contradictory statement takes with one hand and gives away with the other. A tautology is, in virtue of its definitional form, necessarily true. One way to think of tautologies is as statements of the form AB is A or even stranger, A is A or B is B, for example (A and B are conventional symbols for characteristics of things; AB is a symbol for a conjunction of such properties, for example, redness and triangularity which can occur together as properties of red triangles). "Red barns are red" or "Red is red." Tautologies are strange, empty, trivial statements that we hardly ever have occasion to utter. Even more odd, logical contradictories are *denials* of these ultimately trivial necessities. *Of course,* contradictions are absurd. What they affirm *must* be false, for example that some red things are not red; or that some puppies are not dogs. Indeed in the very strongest sense, it is *impossible* that a contradiction could be true.

Even some contingent statements are unlikely ever to be true. Our analysis of contradictions still leaves us with a universe in which there are many wildly improbable things that are *logically* possible but which nevertheless will not actually happen because "it would take a miracle" for them to happen. It is logically possible for iron bars to float on water, or for ping-pong balls in a table tennis game to be hit so hard that they escape the earth's gravity. It is of course impossible in some other sense for these remarkable things to happen. If they *did* happen, it would be a violation of a law of physics. Thus, we can call such happenings physical impossibilities. Theological writers have often defined miracles, for example, walking on water, as "violations of laws of nature." Similarly, it would be a physical impossibility (hence a miracle) for a physical object to attract another physical object gravitationally with a force directly proportional to their masses and inversely proportional to the *cubes* of the distance between them. (The correct statement of the formula discovered by Newton which is an actual law of nature has the word "square" where I have put "cube.")

There are many other impossible things that are neither logical contradictions nor violations of the laws of nature discovered by scientists. These are happenings beyond our current power to produce or control. It is not a contradiction to say that I high jumped seven feet or ran a mile in 3 3/4 minutes. Neither is it a violation of a law of nature that is credited to me when it is said I jump so high or run so fast. Indeed, we know that such things can happen because they already have been done by others. It is *technically impossible* for me to accomplish such feats, even though it would be no miracle (no violation of a law of nature). Similarly, it is technically impossible, that is, beyond my individual capacities and talents, for me to create atomic fission in the laboratory or to write a novel in Chinese. But it is physically impossible, though logically possible (there is no contradiction in its bare description) for me to give birth to a baby.

There is a commonly made mistake of speaking of one type of impossibility as though it is weaker than the others in the sense of "less impossible." But these are not distinctions among degrees of impossibility, but rather among sources and grounds of impossibility. It would betray a confusion of mind to encourage me in a high jumping contest by shouting to me as the bar is set a hundred feet above the ground: "Fear not. What you are trying to do is only physically (not logically) impossible!"

9

Basic Deductive Logic

POSSIBLE TRUTH VALUE COMBINATIONS

When we do not know whether a given proposition is true or false, it is convenient to say that we do not know its "truth value." This is a useful term of art that enables us conveniently to pose some important questions about valid deductive arguments. There are various combinations of truth values that are possible. The premises will have a truth value (each of them will if there is more than one), and the conclusion will have a truth value, in both cases either true or false. The overall validity of the argument will vary, leading to a larger combination of possibilities. It is essential to understand these combinations and examples of each. The student should not forget that a valid argument can have a false conclusion and an invalid argument can have a true conclusion. Various other combinations are possible. The rules for determining validity remain constant, but individual propositions in premise or conclusion will be true or false depending on the facts. And sometimes (in fact most times) the best way of determining the facts will be to go out and look at the world.

Here are some samples of truth value combinations in the premises and conclusions of valid and invalid arguments.

(1)   True premises; true conclusion; valid argument:

All humans are mortal. (True)

Feinberg is human. (True)

Therefore, Feinberg is a mortal. (True)

(VALID)

(2)   False premises (at least one premise is false); false conclusion; valid argument:

All mammals have wings. (False)

All reptiles are mammals. (False)

Therefore, all reptiles have wings. (False)

(VALID)

(3)   Invalid argument with true premises and a true conclusion:

Chicago is north of Dallas. (True)

Feinberg is mortal. (True)

Therefore, all birds have wings. (True)

(INVALID)

(4) Invalid arguments with only true premises and a false conclusion. (By the very definition of "valid," arguments of this form *cannot be valid*.)

If Rockefeller owned all the gold in Fort Knox, then Rockefeller would be wealthy. (True)

Rockefeller does not own all the gold in Fort Knox. (True)

Therefore Rockefeller is not wealthy. (False)

(INVALID)

(5) Valid arguments with false premises and a true conclusion.

All fish are mammals. (False)

All whales are fish. (False)

Therefore, all whales are mammals. (True)

(INVALID)

(6) Invalid argument with false premises and a true conclusion:

All dogs have wings. (False)

All puppies have wings. (False)

Therefore, all puppies are dogs. (True)

(INVALID)

In summary, a two premise deductive argument may have any of the following truth and validity combinations:

PREMISES	CONCLUSION	ARGUMENT
T	T	VALID
T	T	INVALID
F	F	VALID
F	F	INVALID
F	T	VALID
F	F	INVALID
T	F	MUST BE INVALID

Illustrations have been given of arguments in each of these categories. All combinations are possible except one: *An argument cannot have true premises and a false conclusion and still be valid*. But a valid argument can go from false to false, from true to true, or from false to true, and an invalid argument can be in any of these categories, without restriction.

VALIDITY AND SOUNDNESS

A final bit of logical terminology, implicit in the sections preceding it, will be useful. The philosophers who "do logic" never speak of statements or propositions as "valid" or "invalid." These evaluative terms apply to arguments, not to the propositions out of which arguments are constructed. Speaking very generally, valid arguments are logically correct arguments, having premises and conclusions as their constituent parts. In writing a philosophical essay, of course, you want to show that your conclusion is not only supported in the strongest possible ways, but that the premises that provide that support are themselves "reasonably assumed" or shown to be true. In the previous section I considered using an old illustrative valid argument with false premises whose conclusion is: "therefore all reptiles have wings." Once, a student complained to her biology professor about my transmitting false accounts of biological facts. She never quite understood what logic is!

A particular proposition is true or false depending on what the facts happen to be. If you are trying to classify a given argument and you would like to know whether "some fish have wings" is T or F, you must look at books about fish or otherwise consult biologists. Logic can only tell you whether a given set of premises has a certain relationship—logical validity—to the biological proposition. It is easy for any student with a gift of imagination to give a valid argument in support of a false biological proposition, say: "All whales are mammals (T); all mammals have wings (F); therefore all whales have wings (F)." If the premises are true, then the conclusion must be true; but that doesn't help you much if some or all of the premises of the argument, as in this case, are false.

Ideally, what we need if logic is to be practical are arguments that are both valid and have *true* premises. The conclusion of such an argument cannot be false. Logicians call such an argument, "sound." We can thus define soundness as validity plus truth (of the premises). One of the most common ways in which philosophers criticize one another is to concede that the other person's argument is logically impeccable but to insist that some or all of her premises are false.

DEFINITION OF TRUTH FUNCTIONAL CONNECTIVES

Some propositions contain other propositions as components. These propositions are called "compound." Propositions that are not compound are called "simple propositions." Thus—"Roses are red" and "Violets are blue" are both simple propositions, but if we connect them with the word "and" we thereby generate the compound proposition "Roses are red and violets are blue." The truth or falsity of the compound depends, of course, on the truth or falsity of its two simple components, and also on the effect the word "and" has when those components are conjoined. The word "and" is called a conjunction and is expressed by a dot (·) in logical symbolism. If two simple statements are abbreviated by the letters "p" and "q," then the compound proposition which results (p · q) is called a "conjunction" or "the conjunction of p and q."

Conjunction is one of four types of so-called "truth functional connectives" most frequently studied by logicians. The others are negation, whose symbol is the tilde, "~", disjunction (symbolized by the wedge, ∨), and implication (symbolized by the horseshoe, ⊃). Connectives are called truth functional since the question of whether a compound statement is true or false depends on whether the simple components are themselves true or false, and nothing else.

A compound proposition whose components are conjunctively connected is rendered in symbolism as "p · q." Depending on the truth value of the simple component propositions, p and q, there are four possible truth values of the conjunction of p and q. If p is true and q is true, then p · q is true. If p is true and q is false then (p · q) is false. If p is false and q is true, then (p · q) is false. Finally, if p is false and q also is false, then (p · q) is false. The formal definition of (p · q) then is given in what is called a "truth table," a chart that embodies our understanding of the combinations of truth values of simple statements as connected by the truth functional connective being defined.

Thus, the following truth table defines conjunction:

p	q	p · q
T	T	T
T	F	F
F	T	F
F	F	F

In other words, in order for the conjunction of two simple propositions to be true, both simple components must be true.

The truth table for negation is even simpler:

p	~p (not p)
T	F
F	T

In other words, whichever truth value p has, ~p has the other one.

In modern English, the word "or" is ambiguous. In a weak or inclusive sense "p or q" means (p and/or q), "either or both." This is the "or" used in the question "Do you want cream or sugar in your coffee?"—it allows for the possibility that you prefer both cream and sugar. In a strong or exclusive sense "p or q" means "one or the other but not both." The question "Do you want coffee or tea?" is an example of an exclusive "or." The latter is the logician's sense that is captured in the following truth table:

p	q	p ∨ q (p or q)
T	T	T
T	F	T
F	T	T
F	F	F

In other words the disjunction of p and q is false when but only when both disjuncts are false. If it is false that I want coffee and false that I want tea, then it cannot be true that I want either coffee or tea. If at least one disjunct is true then the whole disjunction is true.

The fourth truth functional connective is that expressed by the English words "if . . . then . . . ." in one of their meanings. One of the examples of a proposition of this form is: "If it rains then the grass gets wet." This statement is logically equivalent to the statement, "It cannot be true that it rains and the grass does *not* get wet. Taking the two statements as identical, philosophers proceed to define the connective they call "material implication" by the following truth table that applies to both "p ⊃ q" and to "~(p · ~q)," which behaves logically the same as p ⊃ q. (The conjunction of p with the denial of q cannot be true.)

1	2	3	4	5	6
p	q	~q	p · ~q	~(p · ~q)	p ⊃ q
T	T	F	F	T	T
T	F	T	T	F	F
F	T	F	F	T	T
F	F	T	F	T	T

The first two columns lay out all the possible truth combinations of p and q. They are called "guide columns." The third column is filled in by a similar list of combinations of the truth values in column 2. Then column 4 is filled in by reference to columns 1 and 3. The fifth column then lists the combinations of the truth values in column 4, and since column 5 derives from the mere negation of the values in column 4, it is a simple matter of listing for all combinatory values of 4 the denial of those truth values in column 5. The sixth column, then, when translated back into English, can be seen to be equivalent to the fifth column: "If it rains then the ground gets wet" is identical to "It cannot, or will not, rain without the grass getting wet."

Compound propositions containing the "if . . . then . . ." relation are also commonly called "conditional statements" or "hypothetical statements." The part of the compound normally following the "if " is called the "antecedent." The part following the "then" is called the "consequent." A conditional statement asserts that the truth of the antecedent is a sufficient condition for the truth of the consequent, that *if* the antecedent is true then the consequent is true. Another way of saying this is that the antecedent "implies" or "entails" the consequent, or that the consequent "follows" from the antecedent.

The truth table for implication includes columns for negation and conjunction, and therefore gives the student practice at manipulating symbols of more than one truth functional connective at a time. The role of implication in our reasoning becomes complicated and subtle in advanced logic and we cannot therefore follow it very far in that direction, but we can point out that to say that p implies q is to say that it cannot be the case that p is true and q is false. It is essential to the idea that "if p then q" that you cannot have p and also *not* have q. The one proposition implies the other. The symbolism ~(p · ~q) says that it cannot be the case that p is true and q is not true.

NECESSARY AND SUFFICIENT CONDITIONS

We can use concepts of necessary and sufficient conditions to relate propositions to one another, or we can use them to talk about events and states of affairs outside the world of logic and language. If we do the latter we may not mention "p" or "q" at all, preferring instead to talk directly about events and states of affairs themselves. Thus we can say such things as "if it rains any more tonight then the football field will be muddy tomorrow at game time" which means that more rain will be sufficient to bring about more mud or "only if someone pulls the switch will the light come on" which means that pulling the switch is necessary for lighting the room. There is usually many more than one condition that is necessary for some result, so that if these necessary conditions are *all* satisfied then that will be sufficient to produce the result.

There are many equivalent ways of saying that one thing is necessary for another. Such statements do not always use the vocabulary of logic, but they can always be shown to have the same logical form: (if p then q), or (~(p . ~q)), or (only if p, then q). Lawyers speak of necessary conditions as "but for conditions," that is, conditions *but for which* an event to be explained would not have occurred. Sometimes lawyers resort to the ancient Latin expression, *conditio sine qua non,* "a condition without which not." It should be noted carefully that *if p is necessary for q, then q is sufficient for p.* Thus,

An airplane flies only if there is gas in its tank.

is equivalent to—

If this airplane flies, then there is gas in its tank.

Imagine yourself at the airport. You have been very worried that your visiting friends' plane is out of gas. You are convinced that gas in the tank is necessary if he is to fly home. When you get to the airport he climbs into the plane and takes off. You could say—wouldn't you?—that "There must have been gas in the tank. The fact that the plane is flying is sufficient to show that there was gas in the tank."

In general, if p is a sufficient condition for q, then q is a necessary condition for p. And if p is a necessary condition for q, then q is a sufficient condition for p. But this is not always the case. The presence of oxygen in the air is a necessary condition for fire but not a sufficient condition, since there can be oxygen without fire. There can also be a sufficient condition that is not a necessary condition. Heavy cigarette smoking may well be sufficient to cause lung cancer, but it is not necessary, since nonsmokers sometimes get lung cancer too.

VALID DEDUCTIVE ARGUMENT FORMS:
A SAMPLER

Determining the validity or invalidity of a deductive argument is a matter of form, not of content. Determining the truth or falsity (the truth value) of the propositions that make up the premises of an argument is not a matter of logical forms. If you want to know whether "all bears have wings," read a biology book, or rely on your own memory or common sense. Logic as such is not interested in such matters. If you come to the study of logic already armed with many beliefs of your own about biology, geography, history, or arithmetic, your prior beliefs may be part of a test for validity that you can apply to an argument. If "Bears have wings" is the conclusion or a premise of an argument being tested, it is totally beside the point that bears are misdescribed, if we are interested only in testing the argument. If the doubtful claim in bear biology is the conclusion of the argument, that matters not. If we are testing validity we are asking whether an argument of this form could ever derive a false proposition like the bear-biology claim from a true premise. And of course it would help us if we knew on independent grounds whether that premise is true or false. The argument *must* be invalid, we can conclude, only in that case where the false bear-conclusion is said to follow logically from a premise in whose truth you have great confidence.

There are a number of well-studied logical patterns that exhibit the forms of the leading categories of deductive validity. Let us begin a brief sketch of these formal patterns with those that have a conditional statement as a premise.

Strictly speaking, any set of propositions whose premises are simply irrelevant to its conclusion is an invalid argument. So any argument properly symbolized as (p, q, therefore g) is invalid. Whatever the truth values of p and q and g, they have has no logical bearing on one another. So if p is the proposition "All mammals are quadrupeds," and q is the proposition "Some millionaires are neurotic," then p and q have no relation to one another. They are not even talking about the same thing. Then if g is the proposition that objects attract one another with a force that is directly proportional to their masses and inversely proportional to the square of the distances between them, we have an argument that consists of three true propositions totally irrelevant to one another. The premises can give no support to the conclusion, so that if we interpret an argument as a claim that such support is given, that claim must be rejected and the argument declared invalid. Moreover, it will be easy to invent an argument of the same form (p, q, ∴ g) in which the premises are true and the conclusion false. No valid argument can contain that combination of truth values. Consider then the following argument consisting of mutual irrelevancies:

p, q, ∴ g, where
p = some birds have wings (T)

q = some millionaires are neurotic (T)

g = Dallas is north of Chicago (F)

Here the argument is shown to be invalid because of mutual irrelevancy. It is the sort of argument which is commonly called a "non sequitur" ("not following"). In our example then, p and q, the premises, are both true and the conclusion is false. So the argument must be invalid.

The more interesting fallacies (invalid arguments) have component propositions whose truth values are indeed relevant to one another but whose recognizable forms determine that the conclusion necessarily does not follow from the premises. These are standard argument forms, so common and familiar that they have their own names.

Some of the standard deductive argument forms are valid, guaranteeing that any actual argument that has that form is valid—if its premises are true then its conclusion cannot be false. Other standard argument forms are invalid, that is such that any actual argument with p's and q's filled in can be spotted immediately as invalid. Some arguments in each of these categories employ a conditional statement as a premise. Some have standard forms easily confused with the valid ones, but are actually fallacious (always invalid). Needless to say, it is important to learn how to recognize these forms and learn how to distinguish at first sight the always valid ones from the fallacies, just as in mushroom hunting, it is important to know how to distinguish the fatally poisonous specimens from the innocuous ones.

Let us begin then with a pair of standard valid forms and the poisonous counterparts often confused with them. The first of these was given the Latin name **modus ponens** by medieval logicians, a name still used. An argument has this form when its component propositions are related as follows:

If p then q

p

Therefore, q

Formulated in conventional symbolism, it appears as follows:

p ⊃ q

p

∴ q

It is not difficult to see intuitively that this argument form is always valid. If an argument of this form has true premises, as is sometimes the case, then the conclusion must be true. For example:

If this horse's leg is broken, then he will be mercifully shot.

This horse's leg is broken.

Therefore, this horse will be mercifully shot.

If the premises of this argument are true (as they could easily be, depending on what the facts are) then it is logically necessary that the conclusion is true too. If the conclusion is false then it must be because one or more premise is false. It cannot be false *because* the argument is invalid; we can see from its form alone that it is valid.

If your intuition needs a boost, however, we can use the method of truth tables to test for validity. Begin by listing in the first two vertical columns the possible combinations of truth values between the propositions p and q. There are four such combinations: p and q might both be true; p might be true and q false; q might be true and p false; or both might be false.

p	q	p ⊃ q
T	T	T
T	F	F
F	T	T
F	F	T

Now recall the definitions given earlier of truth functional connectives, particularly of the horse shoe symbol and the connective "if . . . then . . ." (material implication). When p ⊃ q, and p (the two premises) are both true (in the first horizontal row) there the conclusion (q) is also true. There is no possible combination that yields true premises and a false conclusion. Thus, *modus ponens,* the form of this argument, is valid. A more revealing name for *modus ponens* is "the assertion of the antecedent." An argument that qualifies for that description is always valid.

Similarly, the argument whose traditional Latin name is **modus tollens** employs a conditional statement as a key premise and consists in the denial of the consequent. Its form is:

If p then q
Not-q
Therefore, not p

In conventional symbolism,

p ⊃ q (p implies q)
~q
∴ **~p**

The alternative (English) name of this perfectly valid form is "denying the consequent."

That this form is valid is shown by another truth table, this one employing the definition of negation as well as the definition of implication, as follows:

p	q	p ⊃ q	~q	~p
T	T	T	F	F
T	F	F	T	F
F	T	T	F	T
F	F	T	T	T

First, vertical columns are added for not-q, and not-p. That is done easily since the negation of a proposition is simply the proposition whose truth value is the opposite one. If p is true, then not-p is false, and if not-p is false, then p is true. The premises in the argument are (~q) and (p ⊃ q), and the conclusion (~p), vertical columns 4, 3, and 5 respectively. Only in the bottom horizontal line do we have the possible combination in which each premise is true, and in that line the conclusion is true also. So there is not a possible combination in which the premises are true and the conclusion false. So this argument form is valid.

All actual arguments of the forms *modus ponens* and *modus tollens* must be valid. But now we come to the masquerade ball, at which counterfeits for *modus ponens* and *modus tollens* pose as valid arguments, though in fact they are standard fallacies with standard names, and always invalid. The names are given this time only in English, namely **affirming the consequent** and **denying the antecedent**. The former is rendered as follows:

If p then q
q
Therefore, p

94

or in symbolism

$p \supset q$

q

$\therefore p$

For example:

If Rockefeller owns all the gold in Fort Knox, then he is rich.

Rockefeller is rich.

Therefore, Rockefeller owns all the gold in Fort Knox.[1]

Note that the example has true premises and a false conclusion, and therefore must be invalid. The student can help herself appreciate this point by constructing a truth table, as before.

The second fallacious argument form mentioned above is **denying the antecedent.** It can be formulated as follows:

If p then q

Not p

Therefore, not q

Or in symbolism—

$p \supset q$

$\sim p$

$\therefore \sim q$

For example—

If Rockefeller owns all the gold in Fort Knox, then he is rich.

Rockefeller does not own all the gold in Fort Knox. Therefore, Rockefeller is not rich.

The student should make sure that he understands why these forms are valid or invalid, as the case may be, and then implant in himself the habit of knowing instantly which is which. Remember—

Affirming the antecedent (*modus ponens*) is always valid.

Denying the consequent (*modus tollens*) is also always valid. But—

Denying the antecedent is always invalid.

Affirming the consequent also is always invalid.

---

[1] I borrow this alluring example from Irving M. Copi and Keith Burgess-Jackson, *Informal Logic* (Upper Saddle River: Prentice-Hall, 1995), 3rd edition, p. 55.

There are various other forms of deductive argument in which a crucial premise is a conditional statement (if p then q). For example, there is the intuitively obvious valid form called the **hypothetical syllogism.** The name no doubt derives from the prominent role played in it by hypothetical (that is, conditional) propositions. In conventional symbolism, this can be formulated thus—

p ⊃ q

q ⊃ r

∴ p ⊃ r

Note that all three component propositions are conditional. An example—

If Witherspoon wins the next primary election, he will win the nomination.

If Witherspoon wins the nomination, he will win the presidential election.

Therefore, if Witherspoon wins the next primary election, he will win the presidency.

Again a truth table applying the definition of "implication" can be constructed to confirm the validity we sense intuitively in arguments of this form.

Finally, we come to the **constructive dilemma.** Most students enjoy reading the history of the use of arguments of this form because it has always been a favorite of debaters and politicians, and has accumulated dramatic terminology and legendary anecdotes. An argument has the form of a constructive dilemma when it can be formulated as follows:

If p then q and if r then s

p or r

Therefore, q or s

or in conventional symbolism,

(p ⊃ q) . (r ⊃ q)

p or r

∴ q

or

(p ⊃ q) . (r ⊃ s)

p or r

∴ q or s

Arguments of this form, when they are also part of arguments in the sense of quarrels or disagreements, are aimed at putting one's opponent in a dilemma or over a barrel. The arguer reduces his opponent's options to two and then shows how each of these has unacceptable consequences. Often it is the same unacceptable consequence for both options, so the argument in effect demonstrates that the threatened consequences are not only unacceptable, they are also inescapable.

For example, in the middle ages criminal guilt was sometimes determined through trial by ordeal. An inquisitor was in a position to argue to a "witch" or a heretic as follows: "We will attach weights to you and throw you into deep water. Either you will sink or you will swim. If you sink you will soon die painfully. If you swim that will prove that you are guilty of unnatural, witch-like behavior, so we will recapture you and inflict painful death on you as a punishment. Therefore you will soon die painfully." Students of logic over the centuries have spoken of the various ways of responding to it. We must begin by acknowledging the formal validity of this argument. That means that if we are to escape the conclusion it must be because at least one of the premises is false. One possibility is to deny the disjunctive premise. That strategy is called "going between the horns." Another strategy is to deny one of component parts of the major conjunctive premise. That is sometimes called "grasping the argument by one of its horns." In either case one avoids being impaled on the horns of the dilemma either by escaping between the horns or by grasping one of the horns firmly.

Where the threatened harm is the same, no matter which "option" is chosen by the "victim," the form of the argument is somewhat different, but not significantly so. Thus, in the trial by ordeal example, painful death is the unwanted evil in both outcomes. So we might symbolize the argument thus:

(p ⊃ q) . (~p ⊃ q)

p ∨ ~p

∴ q

The disjunctive premise here has the form of a tautology. It cannot possibly be false, so we do not have the option of going "between the horns."

We must also allow that some logical dilemmas have a kind of optimistic ring to them. They are not all polemical, gloomy, or threatening. So, for example, consider the famous arguments of Epicurus (314–270 B.C.E.) that the fear of death is irrational:

> So death, the most terrifying of ills, should mean nothing to us, since so long as we exist, death is not with us, and when death comes, then we do not exist. It should trouble neither the living nor the dead, since where the living person is, death is not, and where death is, the living are not.[2]

We can outline the argument as follows:

---

[2]Epicurus, "Letter to Menoeceus," *Letters, Principal Doctrines, and Vatican Sayings* (Indianapolis: Bobbs-Merrill, 1964), p. 55.

First premise: Since those who are already dead, being unconscious, suffer nothing, they do not suffer death.

Second premise: Those who are still living have not suffered death.

Third, disjunctive premise: Everyone is either living or dead.

First conclusion: Therefore, no one suffers death.

Second conclusion: Therefore, no one should fear death.

The argument form is clearly that of the dilemma:

$$p \supset \sim q$$
$$\sim p \supset \sim q$$
$$p \vee \sim p$$
$$\therefore \sim q$$

The argument is valid, but the first two premises are controversial. The disjunctive premise, however, cannot be doubted. In virtue of its form alone it must be true.

Compare Cicero's equally optimistic emphasis in his wording of a dilemmatic argument against the fear of death—"If souls survive death, then they will be happy, if they perish with death, they do not exist to be unhappy."[3] ($p \supset q; \sim p \supset q; p \vee \sim p; \therefore q$)

[3]Cicero, *Tusc. Quest.* i, as quoted by W.E.H. Lecky, *History of European Morals.* (New York: George Braziller, Inc., 1955), Vol. II, p. 205.

10

Logic Without Necessity

INFORMAL FALLACIES

We can mean by the word "fallacy" any instance of incorrect reasoning. That would include an enormous miscellany of reasoning errors that have no particular form except that their premises are irrelevant to their conclusions. Instead of giving these fallacies some standard name and defining structure, we could simply call them all "fallacies of irrelevance," and give them all one symbolic structure reflecting their irrelevance. Or we could apply to them all one impressive Latin name that emphasizes the ground of their invalidity, say *non sequitur* or (better) *ignoratio elenchi* ("irrelevant conclusion"). But this category is overcrowded with specimens, not to mention that *all* fallacies, in a sense, are fallacies of irrelevance. The point is that some invalid arguments have a clear, recognizable form, easy to symbolize, that permits us to treat them as a particular standardized mistake. But other fallacious arguments, instead of having specialized structures uniquely their own, have a sort of formlessness that does not clearly distinguish them from other invalid arguments, like p ⊃ q, q, ∴ r. We can continue to do what we started in the last chapter and give all arguments that consist (say) of three mutually irrelevant propositions with the arbitrary symbolic form: p, q, ∴ r. But in a way, that symbolism is not precise enough to qualify as a specific fallacy with its own name.

There are reasoning mistakes, however, that have more memorable structures, and more capacity to persuade. Many of these are very effective persuaders (in the cant of the underworld, handguns used to be called "persuaders"). But if the claim is made that these arguments "work" or "go through," and that therefore they cannot be "mistakes" or "errors," this is to make a mistake about these mistakes. Whether an argument is fallacious or not is a matter of fact. If someone says," I will give you a box of candy if you come to my house," then he issues an invitation or makes an offer. What he says does not become an *argument,* just because one of its sentences is conditional in form. If the speaker goes on to claim that he has "proved" something, he is mistaken again. He did not even argue, much less argue validly. In this respect, the speaker's remarks join several other standard persuasive devices common enough to have fixed names, and Latin names at that. Suppose that one party, *A*, trying to persuade another party, *B*, to do or to believe something, requests, implores, demands, or threatens her with the aim of persuading her to do or believe that thing. It would be a bad mistake on the theoretical level to infer from the fact that the persuasion has succeeded that it was a "successful argument," and therefore a valid one, or to infer from the fact that the persuasion failed to persuade that it was an "unsuccessful argument," and therefore an invalid or fallacious one. A third party, C, who is a philosophical observer of the primary transaction between A and B, himself commits a kind of "fallacy" at the theoretical level if he confuses a use of language that is meant to persuade another party with a claim to have demonstrated some truth, or confuses its success with logical validity. This group of "informal fallacies," as they are sometimes called, includes, among many others, the following:

The standard name *argumentum ad baculum* is applied to an effort to persuade by threatening force: "If you don't say what I want you to say (or believe or do what I want you to believe or do, as the case may be), then I will beat the hell out of you," is obviously not an argument. If it were, I suppose it would have to have the following form:

If you don't admit that p, then I will beat you up. (sole premise)
Therefore, p.

It may be that your threat gives me a good reason for saying that I believe that p, but that is quite another thing from saying that the credibility of your threat is evidence for p, or that it implies or entails or proves that p. In fact it is wholly irrelevant to p. A person of ordinary prudence who is persuaded by fear of the threatener's superior size, strength, and pugilistic prowess, may admit, at the moment the blows begin, that he has just been given some "reasons," even some good reasons, for acting as demanded, though he has been given no reason supporting p, no reason for changing his belief to the one demanded, even if it were possible to do so.

The heroic philosopher, if she were in the position of the threatened party, might persist in her claim that her threatener is committing the *argumentum ad baculum,* and that the *argumentum ad baculum* truly is a fallacy. If she is heroic enough, she might even finish her defiant remarks with a Kantian flourish, saying that as a rational being he will not accept reasons as irrelevant as these." Oh yeah?" replies her powerful but illogical tormentor. "I will now prove how irrational philosophers like you really are, for all your so-called heroism. Here is the most cogent of all my arguments." And suiting his action to his words, he takes a gun out of his pocket and shoots the philosopher dead. So logic and rationality may be at odds in certain circumstances. Our topic is logic.

Another set of "arguments" confusing persuasive efficacy with validity bears the Latin name *argumentum ad miseracordium,* and it is every bit as much an informal fallacy as the *argumentum ad baculum.* Consider the undergraduate student in tears who complains to her professor about the "unfairness" of her grade. The grade of B in his course, she says, did not do her justice. She deserved an A given the special circumstances that she has applied to medical school, and if she is not admitted, the disappointment will ruin her life and break her parents' hearts. *Therefore* she deserves an A and her professor has the duty of changing her present grade to an A. The word "Therefore" is the sign that a conclusion is about to be stated, and supported by reasons stated in the premises. In effect the argument says: "You owe me an A, because I and others will be disappointed and heart-broken if you do not make the change I am begging you for." The verdict: invalid!

SOME INDUCTIVE INFERENCES, GOOD AND BAD

In writing your philosophical paper, you will probably have more occasions to use inductive arguments than deductive ones. If you employ only arguments that claim to establish with necessity their conclusions, your pages are likely to look more like high school geometry exercises, with pages cluttered with symbolic notation (perhaps), every assertion boldly unqualified and often seeming dogmatic in consequence. Geometrical proofs and mathematical demonstrations rarely use words like "maybe" and "perhaps." Humanize your paper by making it seem to be the voice of a real flesh and blood person, not that of the eternal verities booming from on high. You want to be able to say "sometimes" not only "always," "some things," as well as "all" and "none." A careful philosopher will claim only that she has "given some reasons" for her conclusion, or presented part of the case for it, admitting that important work remains to be done. It is hard humanizing your paper if you use only arguments that are deductive in form, claiming that their conclusions follow "necessarily," or declaring your own psychological certainty of their truth.

There are numerous tasks in life that require reasonable persons to "give reasons for" rather than prove, demonstrate, or render certain. Law courts are a familiar example. In the criminal law, for instance, a defendant cannot be convicted unless the jury believes that she behaved as charged and believes further that her guilt, while neither logically necessary, nor psychologically certain, is nevertheless pretty strong evidence, so strong that it is "beyond a reasonable doubt." And yet the argument in the mind of the jury does not involve exclusive use of deduction. Inductive arguments too can carry conviction. Instead of logical necessity, the inductive argument (by definition) purports to show the probability of certain vital propositions that would lead a reasonable person in the direction of belief. A reasonable person, indeed, would not even be *able* to doubt it. In other branches of the law, the required evidence is somewhat weaker but still strong, for example reasons that are "clear and compelling," conclusions that are "highly probable," "more probable than not," or "plausible." Subtle differences in these criteria would be lost in a paper that recognizes only deductive "necessity."

Inductive arguments, however, are no more immune from mistakes, and although inductive mistakes are less commonly labeled "fallacies," they can be as destructive to the reasoning processes as those mistakes that *are* called fallacies. A few samples will suffice. Inductive arguments play an important part in ascriptions of causation to events, in explanations, predictions, and opinion surveys, among other things. Where inductive reasoning gives us the opportunity to go right in these activities, it usually offers the opportunity also—and the temptation—to go wrong. Consider the famous argument *post hoc ergo propter hoc* ("after the fact, therefore because of the fact"). One commits this mistake in reasoning when one attributes the cause of a given event to another event that came earlier, for the sole apparent reason that it *did* come earlier. This mistake is made so frequently in political debates that one might almost call it the basic argument of democratic politics, except for the fact that it is almost always used against the incumbent candidate, holding him responsible for what has happened "during his watch." Did the Ohio River flood during his presidency? Then his election or the policies he pursued must have been the cause. It is enough to show that prices on the stock market fell during his term of office to show (allegedly with high probability) that his policies caused the decline. Were we at peace before he assumed office and at war later? It must be because his actions caused it. But incumbents can and do use this weak argument too. Are you better off now than you were under the previous president? If so, that shows that this president's policies have worked. Actually what facts of this sort "prove" is that the speaker's inductive logic is not to be trusted.

BEGGING THE QUESTION

Medieval logicians, who wrote in Latin, had their own fancy name for our next fallacy: a "*petitio principii.*" English speakers too have other names for it—a "circular argument" and "begging the question." Technically, a circular argument can be defined as an argument that assumes in its premises the conclusion it claims to be proving. That procedure makes the reasoner's task altogether too easy to do her any good. She argues in a circle when she uses her premises to prove (or otherwise support) her conclusion, and uses her conclusion in the proof of one of her premises. The circularity fallacy brings to mind the two persons, Mr. A and Ms. B, who apply at a bank for a loan. First Mr. A asks for a loan. The banker asks him if there is anyone who can testify to his honesty and trustworthiness. At that point, Mr. A introduces his friend Ms. B to the banker. Ms. B then recommends Mr. A, declaring him to be absolutely truthful and trustworthy. "Very good," says the banker to Mr. A. "Your friend Ms. B has given us a very good testimonial in your behalf. Now all we need to know is whether Ms. B is herself truthful and trustworthy. Who can recommend her? "No problem," replies Mr. A. "*I* will recommend her." And so we have a circle. We learn that A can be trusted on the authority of B, who can be trusted on the authority of A.

In philosophy a circular argument often takes the same form. A conclusion is supported on someone's authority, and that authority is derived logically from an argument one of whose tacit premises is the very proposition that is meant to be proved. The standard example in logic texts is a particular kind of religious fundamentalism. "We can know that God exists," the argument proceeds, "because the bible tells us so." "Yes, but how do you know that the bible is true?" asks the critic of this particular argument. "No problem," the proof-giver replies, "The bible must be true because it is the word of God." The proof-giver has begged the question.

Put more formally, an argument is offered to prove p. A key premise in that argument is q. So the argument at this point is: q /∴ p. Let us suppose that this is a valid argument, but that we can't tell whether it is sound until we learn whether its premise, q, is true. So we come up with another valid argument: p /∴ q. So now we have completed two arguments, one proving p, our immediate objective, and the other proving q, which is a premise in the argument for p. But the argument for q uses p as a premise in its own proof. In order to show that p is true, we have to assume that p is true!

An interesting thing about circular arguments is that although they are fallacies in the very broad sense of "mistaken reasoning," they are not fallacies in the narrow sense of "invalidity." In fact a circular argument is actually a *valid* argument in the logician's technical sense of "valid." Assuming itself in its own proof may make the circular argument a poor argument, but no more an *invalid* one than any

argument of the form: p ∴ p. An argument of this sort will not advance our knowledge any beyond what is represented in the premise, but it doesn't lead us necessarily into false conclusions from true premises either, as say the assertion of the consequent or denial of the antecedent do. Nevertheless, begging the question is a bad way to reason.

ANALOGICAL REASONING

Inductive inference is an important part of scientific methodology. In addition to these forms of reasoning, there are inductive arguments on a variety of subjects, many of which are found in works of philosophy. The inductive arguments that have interested philosophers most are probably arguments from analogy. Analogical reasoning has been central to the historical debates over the "argument from design" in the philosophy of religion.[1] It is also the form of argument some philosophers have used in their attempts to determine whether or not "lower animals" can reason or feel pain. And analogical arguments have been frequently examined in the philosophical efforts to reconstruct our knowledge of physical objects, other minds, and the uniformity of nature.

---

[1]See William Paley in *Reason and Responsibility*, 15th edition (Boston, MA Wadsworth, 2014), Part 1, and David Hume, *ibid*.

Analogical arguments promise neither necessity nor certainty. There is therefore no simple litmus test for validity when confronted by them, but only criteria of appraisal. Analogies come in many sizes and can be exchanged for analogies that are stronger, weaker, closer, more distant, more or less complete. Analogies are similarities. Analogical arguments are inferences from present similarities to additional similarities whose existence might be inferred from the analogies close at hand. The form of an argument from analogy is as follows:

> Entity A has attributes $a, b, c,$ and z.
> Entity B has attributes $a, b, c.$
> Therefore, entity B probably has attribute z also.[2]

Better and worse arguments of this form can readily be imagined. Instead of four individuals (a, b, c, d), we might compare 25 individuals (a, b, c . . . z). Instead of attributes p, q, r, we might examine p, q, r, s, t. These and similar ways of strengthening the central analogies make the conclusion more probable.

If the student wishes to discover or invent criteria of appraisal for analogical arguments, there is no better place to start than with the eighteenth century debate between William Paley and David Hume, which centers on the closeness or distance of the analogy between works of design and craftsmanship, like boats, houses, and watches, on the one hand, and the whole experienced world, on the other. A paper on this subject that finds room for a discussion of inferences by analogy, with lots of homey examples of analogical arguments that seem to be good ones, would be a wonderfully appropriate topic. But remember, give arguments.

A SAMPLER OF FALLACIES

There are dozens of standard types of mistakes in reasoning that are called "informal fallacies" and given standard names. One important class of such fallacies are those that confuse the history of a thing's development with an analysis of the thing it has become. Under the influence of the theory of evolution in biology, we now expect investigation to disclose that even the most complex of living organisms is the culmination of millions of years of change and development out of much simpler ancestors. The evolutionary process, of course, demands the most careful study, but the use of what C.D. Broad called the "genetic method" in philosophy carries a grave danger. Broad, a distinguished philosopher in the 1920s and 1930s at Cambridge University, coined the term "the genetic fallacy" to refer to the mistake

---

[2]Hurley, P. J. A *Concise Introduction to Logic.* 11th edition (Boston: Wadsworth, 2012), p. 509.

likely to be made by incautious users of the genetic method.[3] Supposing that we are trying to formulate a philosophical theory of some characteristic human activity or institution, for example "institutional religion." Call whatever we are studying "A." "[W]e learn that A developed into B, B into C, and C into the thing in question."[4] The first step in the genetic fallacy is to pounce on one of the earlier factors that is only a trivial necessary condition for the thing to be analyzed, and treat it as if it were an important sufficient condition. Broad cites writers in the Freudian school of psychology who have sometimes claimed that the activity or institution in question would not have come into existence *but for* (note this sign of a necessary condition) the suppression of sexual feeling.

The second step in the fallacy is to take the relatively trivial necessary condition for the thing being analyzed, and conclude that the one is *nothing but* the other "in a disguised form."[5] The following is an example of the full fallacy in both steps:

◆ **Suppressed sexual desire is a necessary condition for a taste for music;[6] therefore a taste for music is nothing but a disguised form of sexual desire.**

The "full fallacy," as I will call it, contains these two errors plus even a third. They are (1) confusing an important sufficient condition for a thing with a relatively trivial necessary condition for that thing, (2) confusing a history of the becoming of a thing with an analysis of the thing it has become; (3) confusing the thing to be analyzed with a corrupted, defective, or inferior version of the "ancestor" it has evolved from, which is to treat the end (of a long historical process) as "just the beginning in disguise."[7] Broad gives the following example of the genetic fallacy in its full form:

◆ **(1) Action from a sense of duty developed out of action from fear of the ghosts of dead ancestors, and (2) this developed out of action from fear of living chiefs. (3) Therefore, the sense of duty as it now exists is just a disguised form of fear of punishment by tribal chiefs.[8]**

---

[3]Broad, C.D. *The Mind and its Place in Nature* (New York: Harcourt, Brace and Company, 1929), pp. 11–14.

[4]*Ibid.*, p. 12.

[5] *Ibid.,* pp. 13 *et passim.*

[6]Broad here refers to the psychological theories of Sigmund Freud and his British disciple, Ernest Jones.

[7]Broad, op. cit. (see note 4), p. 12.

[8]*Ibid.*

Two other informal fallacies exploit the fact that there are two different ways in which an expression can attribute a predicate to a *group* or *collection* of objects. The characteristic in question may attach both to the group as a whole and to each and every member of the group. Alternatively, the predicate may apply to the group but not necessarily to any of its members. In the former case, the attribute is predicated *distributively* to the group (hence to each of its members), and in the latter case *nondistributively*. A reasoner commits the *fallacy of division* when she infers from the fact that a group has a certain characteristic the idea that each member of the group has that characteristic. This sort of transfer from group to individual is a "fallacy" only when the characteristic in question is the kind that is applied to groups *distributively,* like "strong," for example. The following argument, therefore, is fallacious:

✧ **Notre Dame has a powerful football team. John Doe is a member of the Notre Dame football team. Therefore, John Doe is a powerful man.**

Note also that sometimes the facts are such that both premises are true and the conclusion false. That the facts could *ever* lead to that combination of truth values, as we have seen, is impossible in a valid argument.

The *fallacy of composition* is the reverse side of the fallacy of division, where the inference goes from an attribution to an individual member to attribution to a group. An example is the following:

✧ **Socrates is a Greek. Socrates is a philosopher. Therefore, all Greeks are philosophers.**

We have now completed our brief survey of mistakes in reasoning. A full appreciation of the hazards that beset reasoning on every side is produced by the much longer list of "informal fallacies" that have been isolated and given their own names by other writers: *argumentum ad hominem, argumentum ad ignorantiam,* the fallacy of *non causa pro causa,* the fallacy of hasty induction, the fallacy of unrepresentative samples, the *ignoratio elenchi, argumentum ad populum,* the fallacy of *tu quoque,* the fallacy of the red herring, the gambler's fallacy, the pathetic fallacy, and many more.[9]

---

[9]Hurley, Patrick J. A *Concise Introduction to Logic* (Belmont, CA: Wadsworth, 2011), pp. 119-196.

11

Varieties of Philosophy Papers

RULES OF STRATEGY

Readers of this handbook have encountered rules in almost every chapter. In early chapters there were discussions of moral and legal rules. Then came rules of grammar and diction, logic, and even "rules of style," though they are for the most part "rules" in a different sense. There are in fact many different kinds of rules. At least two kinds of rules are associated with *games*. First, there are constitutive rules, so called because games are constituted by these rules. To learn tennis, for example, is to learn what one must do to score points, what moves are recognized as legitimate, what is the scope of an umpire's discretion, what are the prescribed dimensions of the playing surface, and so on. Similarly, if a person wishes to play chess, she must learn to follow rules that invalidate certain movements of the chess pieces. She may not move a rook diagonally; nor may she move a bishop any way but diagonally. A game which assigned different directions to those pieces might be a game equally interesting as chess, but it would not *be* chess, for it would neglect the rules which define what chess is.

A second class of rules also apply with special clarity to games. These are not rules that constitute the game; they are more like pieces of advice about how to get good at the game—how to develop skill, and how to make winning moves. They don't declare what is permitted or what is obligatory. Rather they recommend, from among the techniques and strategies that are permitted, those that are likely to be successful. They are guides toward competitive victory or whatever noncompetitive goal the game may aim at.

MANAGEABLE PHILOSOPHICAL TASKS

A person who unfailingly follows prevailing rules of grammar and diction, who cultivates balance and flow in the interest of easy reading, and who can always recognize and call by name a logical fallacy when she sees one, is prepared *not* to commit writing errors, but until she knows more than that, she is not prepared to write a good paper. To be a good philosophical paper, an essay must do more than avoid errors; it must also manifest positive virtues.

Where are the rules for positive achievement? The student will reasonably ask that question. Moreover, she might also point out, in understandable alarm, that the wisest thinkers produced by our civilization have attempted to prove their philosophical positions, and yet the problems they meant to solve are still with us. The same "isms" contend as in Descartes' time, and the lack of conclusive argument portends more failure of the philosophers to find agreement in the future. How then can a beginning student hope to succeed in argument, where all of the others have failed? How is this possible, especially when the student has not yet had time to compile strategic rules and techniques out of her own limited experience?

The situation is not as bad as it seems. Giving conclusive arguments ("proofs") in support of a philosophical position is indeed an extremely difficult thing to do. But it is not the only sort of thing you might try to do in a philosophy paper. There are some useful philosophic undertakings that are much less difficult than that.

MODEST PARTIAL REASONS

Imagine that you have just completed a paper arguing for some philosophical position. A friendly critic reads it at your invitation, and then in the course of his constructive criticism he complains that you have not proved your conclusion; it might still be false. In reply, perhaps, you clarify your intentions. You didn't mean to find a set of reasons constituting a proof, you say. You are more modest than that. You meant only to add one more reason, however modest it may be in itself, to the case for the position you are supporting. If you argued soundly then you strengthened the case for that position, rendered it more plausible than it may have seemed in a formulation that gave little emphasis to this point. Plausibility, unlike truth, is a matter of degree. You have made a philosophical position more eligible for belief than it formerly seemed, and more eligible for belief now than some of its near rivals. There may of course be many comparable points that can be made on the other side. You do not deny that. You insist only that when the "final score" is tallied up your point goes into the final judgment. That would be a contribution both useful and modest. Perhaps a better analogy would be to a court of law where a case for one verdict must be balanced against a case for an alternative verdict, or where the plaintiff 's case in a civil action must be weighed against the defendant's, and both cases are complex mixtures of reasons. That law courts use the concept of a "proof " so prominently, however, is unfortunate insofar as it suggests some similarity between the work of a prosecutor making her case, and the work of a mathematician proving a theorem. Some classic philosophy has been influenced by mathematics, but for the most part, philosophical reasoning bears more resemblance to "case-making" than to theorem-proving.

INTERPRETATION

Another traditional task of philosophers deviates from the intimidating "proof" model in still another direction. Both "conclusive proofs" on the one hand and more modest case-making on the other are efforts to justify the beliefs that reasoning has been used to support. In the one form of justification, the support is claimed to be partial and tentative, and in the other the support is held to be conclusive, but in both cases the reasoning can be put to use to justify (to render at least more plausible if not certain) a *belief* in the position that has been strengthened. A second task of philosophy departs from these models of *justification,* arguing instead for an *interpretation* of a philosophical doctrine. Note that interpretation is something that contrasts with justification but not with rational argument. All philosophy employs reasoning. It is just that rational argument is employed, in the one case, directly on behalf of a philosophic thesis, and in the other, on behalf of an explanation of what the thesis means, what its supporting argument is, what premises are left implicit, but which must be assumed, how the position being interpreted is logically related to or distinguished from other positions easy to confuse with it, what strategic motive the advocate of the position under consideration has for fitting this somewhat smaller thesis into the more complex web of propositions that forms his system.

Whichever of these approaches are taken, one general methodological assumption should be made. Give the philosopher whose work is under inspection the benefit of the doubt. Select the interpretation of her work that makes the most sense out of it. If one interpretation of a philosopher's work makes it seem silly and a rival interpretation makes it seems sensible, then, other things being equal, the latter is the more plausible interpretation of the two. In that way interpretation and rational justification become intertwined, and the evaluation of philosophical theses becomes part of the process by which they are interpreted. Interpretation, then, can seem to be a very complex business, not at all a "modest" undertaking. But by concentrating on only one facet of the process and claiming only to have given one reason perhaps among many for a particular interpretation, the student-philosopher's task can be reduced to manageable dimensions.

GENERALIZATION AND COUNTEREXAMPLE

Many a philosophical doctrine finds expression as a generalization, e.g. "All S are P." In such cases one could refute the thesis by presenting evidence that some S is not P. If there exists a non-P-ish S, then it is false that all S are P. This way of refuting a generalization is called "refutation by counterexample."

It might seem that the philosopher who is affirming the generalization has a more difficult task than does the philosopher who attacks it. The affirmative position is commonly put quickly on the defensive. The negative position, on the other hand, is often simpler in structure, and its proponent is tempted to be more aggressive. The defender of the generalization may not know how to defend it, and often may assume a great variety of possible sources of the falsehoods. The aggressive party, on the other hand, is led right to the heart of the matter. It is both necessary and sufficient for him to show that there is (or in a more speculative version of their disagreement—that there could be) an S that is not P. If he has an S that is not P hanging in his closet, he need only go get it and show it to his opponent to prove that his opponent's initial position was false.

If they are reasonable persons of good will, the disputing philosophers (or they could be scientists or laymen) will profit from this sort of resolution of their disagreement, for it suggests various paths they might follow in a quest, not for victory, but for truth. Perhaps the counterexample came from a source of such objects that the generalization had failed to consider. Now he knows better, and has a direction to turn in to fill in the gap in his knowledge. Perhaps he will now assert, with reinvigorated confidence, that all S is P except Q, or maybe if the facts become still more complex, "All S is P except those Qs that are not R."

DEFINITION

Many traditional philosophical problems seem to have the form of requests for definitions. Thus there should be no surprise in the fact that many traditional philosophical doctrines actually have the form of definitions or at least of statements that are easily interpreted as, or convertible to, definitions. The ancient Greek philosopher Socrates (470 B.C.–399 B.C.) left us no writing of his own, but his student Plato wrote dialogues in which he gave the major role to Socrates. Socrates is then depicted as a largely unappreciated pest, asking in a tone of mock humility (the famous "Socratic irony") of the most respectable fellow citizens he could find on the streets of Athens such questions as "What is justice?", "What is love?", "What is knowledge?", "What is piety?"—all questions of the form "What is x?" In a sense Socrates' questions could be said to be requests for definitions, since there is but a small step from "What is x?" to "What does 'x' mean?" But there is also a paradox in that idea. Obviously Socrates and his fellow Athenians had a common language in which most of them were fluent, and normally they communicated quite adequately in their "mother tongue." Why then did they need definitions? The ancient Greeks did not have detailed dictionaries. We do, but when we do philosophy in the Socratic manner and ask one another what "justice" means, or what it means for one person to love another, why don't we just look up the words "justice" and "love" in *Webster's Dictionary?*

Since Socrates' philosophical definitions had the form of generalization (to say that justice is x is to say that all and only just things are x, that x is both sufficient and necessary for justice, a kind of double generalization), the dialectic of generalization and counterexample applies to definition too. To be a good definition, then, a philosophical definition should be neither too broad nor too narrow. A statement that defines an X as a Y is too broad if it should turn out that there are some Ys that are not Xs. It is too narrow if there are some Xs that are not Ys. There are thus two kinds of possible counterexamples: Xs that are not Ys, and Ys that are not Xs. That a good definition be neither too broad nor too narrow is a rule applying to dictionary makers as well as to philosophers. If there is a difference between these two groups of definition makers, it is that philosophers want more than that out of their definitions. Somehow they want their definitions (a) to be neither too broad nor too narrow and (b) to express knowledge of a non-linguistic kind that is responsive to our deepest philosophical perplexities. A definition of "human being" should tell us something important about human beings, not merely something useful about the English language.

The inadequacy of purely linguistic criteria for philosophical purposes is well illustrated by the story of the efforts of some of Plato's successors at the Athenian Academy to define "man" (here, meaning "human being"). After much debate, they finally settled on: "Man is a featherless biped," since their investigations had failed to uncover any featherless animal (that is, any nonbird) that had only two legs, nor any two-legged creatures, other than humans, who didn't have feathers. "Man is a featherless biped" seemed to uniquely pick out human beings, which is what any definition of "man" is supposed to do.

Legend has it that the cynic Diogenes (fourth century B.C.E) presented his counterexample in a characteristically dramatic fashion. He plucked a chicken (I assume it was a dead chicken) and threw it over the Academy wall. The Academicians saw quickly that Diogenes had effectively refuted by counterexample the Academic definition. Diogenes' plucked chicken was indeed a featherless biped, but obviously it was not a man, so the definition was too broad.

The Academic philosophers tried to avoid embarrassment by amending their definition. (Actually they could have refuted Diogenes by arguing that definition of biological species must always refer to the characteristics the animals possess while alive. The featherlessness of the counterexample was an "artificial" characteristic acquired by a single member of the species and only after she was dead.) The Academic philosophers soon added "with broad nails" to their refuted definition so that their final conclusion was that a man is a featherless biped with broad nails (as opposed to the claws of birds). All and only human beings are designated by that description. The real point of this ancient tale, however, is that if a definition's only merit is that it lacks certain demerits, namely being too wide or too narrow, then it is likely to impart no philosophic wisdom whatever and to have no bearing on the sources of genuinely philosophic perplexity. For instance, suppose we are debating the moral permissibility of abortion and we decide that we need to know whether the fetus is a human being. Should the breadth of the fetus's nails really play any role in this debate? The sort of definition that is needed to help us think about abortion is some characteristic of humans and only humans that casts a light in our dark place. We need a definition that helps us understand why being human seems to carry a kind of moral weight. A definition that is suitable only for teaching immigrants a new language is not likely to cast the required light.

OTHER CATEGORIES
OF PHILOSOPHICAL PAPERS

A quick survey of the articles that professional philosophers publish, largely for one another, in their professional journals shows how misleading it would be to represent all philosophy as original attempts to prove some doctrine. Some of these articles are critical comparisons of two or more philosophical theories, e.g. Western and Buddhist theories of the self. Sometimes it is useful to compare two theories, listing, point by point, the strengths and weaknesses of two quite different approaches. Other articles adjudicate controversies, sometimes these are disagreements about the truth of a thesis, and other times disagreements between interpretations of an influential writer. Others present a hypothetical counterexample to another philosopher's generalization. If *A* has presented a counterexample to *B*'s generalization, you might come to *B*'s aid by suggesting that she change one small feature of her generalization, thereby evading *A*'s counterexample at small cost. Other papers introduce a new and useful distinction or else undermine an old distinction. You might try to show that, properly interpreted, *A* and *B* "don't really" disagree at all, though they both might think they do. The student should not be reluctant to write "negative" papers pointing out difficulties in another philosopher's arguments. Either that philosopher's conclusion is vulnerable to counter-argument showing it to be false, or there are defects in the argument the writer used in its behalf, in which case it may yet be true, but no reason has been given for believing it is. All of these sorts of papers are genuinely philosophical.

12

Philosophical Research on the Internet

The Internet provides a wealth of resources for students looking to find material to help in writing philosophy papers. This material comes in many forms. Perhaps the most helpful are bibliographies of philosophical works, whole philosophical texts, and philosophical encyclopedias.

A number of sites provide free texts of many philosophical classics. These texts are almost always in the public domain—their copyright has expired, and some good academic citizens have made the effort to store the classic text in digital format. These sources are especially valuable when tracking down English classics; philosophical works in other languages, if freely available on the Internet, are usually offered in old translations that may strike contemporary readers as out of date. Still, free is free, and any student wanting access to a classic at the touch of a keyboard is well-advised to consult some of the sites referred to below.

Perhaps the most valuable Internet resource comes in the form of Internet encyclopedias. There are a small number of them whose content is focused exclusively on philosophy.

Though a quick Internet search on philosophical research will yield a great number of responses, not every site, naturally, is as trustworthy or as useful as others. The sites described below are ones that, as of this printing, are especially reliable and valuable.

General

- Episteme Links (http://www.epistemelinks.com/)
    o An all-purpose site containing links to internet encyclopedias, bibliographies of philosophical works, E-texts (searchable by philosopher's name, book title, and keyword), and discussion groups.

Encyclopedias and Introductory Material

- Stanford Encyclopedia of Philosophy (http://plato.stanford.edu/)
    o An online encyclopedia with in-depth entries on a wide range of philosophical topics.
- Internet Encyclopedia of Philosophy (http://www.iep.utm.edu/)

- o Offers briefer and sometimes more accessible coverage than the Stanford Encyclopedia.
- Philosophy Compass (http://philosophy-compass.com/)
  - o An online-only journal that publishes overviews of the academic literature on various philosophical topics.

Databases and Search Engines

- Philosopher's Index (http://philindex.org/)
  - o A registry, searchable by author, title, subject, date, or keyword, of all major philosophy books and articles published in the last several decades. Most college and university libraries have paid the relevant fees for this service, which does allow for free access to the contents if you are an enrolled student.
- Philpapers (http://philpapers.org/)
  - o A comprehensive index of philosophical papers and books, categorized by topic.
- Google Scholar (http://scholar.google.com/)
  - o Google's search engine for academic documents.

Sites by Area of Philosophy

- History
  - o Early Modern Texts (http://www.earlymoderntexts.com/)
    - ▪ Classic texts in the history of philosophy, "translated" to modern English to render them more accessible. Students should use this site as a complement to, rather than a substitution for, reading the original texts.
- Value Theory
  - o Public Reason (http://publicreason.net/)
    - ▪ A blog for political philosophers.
  - o Oxford Uehiro Centre for Practical Ethics (http://www.practicalethics.ox.ac.uk/)
    - ▪ This site provides ethical analysis of current events.
  - o Ethics Updates (http://ethics.sandiego.edu/)

- A helpful collection of resources and updates on applied ethics and ethical theory.
  - PEA Soup (http://peasoup.typepad.com/)
    - A blog dedicated to Philosophy, Ethics, and Academia.
  - Legal Theory Blog (http://lsolum.typepad.com/)
    - Offers summaries of important views and ideas in the philosophy of law, and announces recent work relevant to legal theory.
- Experimental Philosophy
  - Experimental Philosophy (http://experimentalphilosophy.typepad.com/)
    - Tracks developments in experimental philosophy.
  - The Experimental Philosophy Homepage (http://pantheon.yale.edu/~jk762/ExperimentalPhilosophy.html)
    - Catalogues experimental philosophy papers by topic.
- Metaphysics and Epistemology
  - The Epistemology Research Guide (http://www.ucs.louisiana.edu/~kak7409/Epistemological Research.htm)
    - Links to epistemology course pages, papers, and blogs.

News

- Leiter Reports (http://leiterreports.typepad.com/)
  - Covers news from, and concerning, academic philosophy. The author also edits a popular ranking of philosophy graduate programs, The Philosophical Gourmet Report (http://www.philosophicalgourmet.com/).
- Prophilosophy (http://prophilosophy.wordpress.com/)
  - Another blog with links and discussion of philosophy news.
- The Philosopher's Magazine (http://www.thephilosophersmagazine.com/)
  - An interesting and accessible philosophy magazine that includes interviews, essays, and regular columns.

Professional

- The American Philosophical Association
  (http://www.apaonline.org/)
  - o The major professional organization for philosophers in the
    United States and Canada.
- Philevents (http://philevents.org/)
  - o An announcement page for philosophy talks and conferences,
    including undergraduate conferences.

Appendix

A Checklist for Philosophy Papers

The checklist that appears on the pages that follow is designed to help you evaluate your philosophy paper. As you read over your drafts, consider each of these criteria, and look for ways to improve your topic, use of citations, quotations and attributions, the argument you present, and the quality of your writing.

This checklist is also valuable to guide other readers of your paper. Bring it with you to the writing center at your school so that the reader helping you understands how you are likely to be evaluated or exchange papers with a fellow student and use the checklist to give feedback on each other's papers.

Your instructor may suggest other uses for the checklist, including using it to provide you with feedback, suggestions, or a grade on your paper.

A CHECKLIST FOR PHILOSOPHY PAPERS

Name:
Date:
Title of Paper:

What is your main thesis? (Chapter 1)

_____

_____

_____

_____

_____

What type of paper have you written? (Chapter 11)
- ☐ Argument in support of a position
- ☐ Modest partial reasons supporting a position
- ☐ Interpretation of a reading or philosopher's view
- ☐ Generalization or counterexample
- ☐ Comparison of two positions or theories
- ☐ Analysis of a concept

Read your paper to evaluate how well it meets each of these criteria:
Topic (Chapters 1, 3)
The chosen topic is appropriate for the assignment.
The level of difficulty of the topic is appropriate for the assignment.

Citations, quotations, and attributions (Chapter 2)
Citations are handled consistently in the appropriate style.
Plagiarism has been strictly avoided.

Argument (Chapters 3, 8, 9, 10)

The question, problem or topic has been stated clearly at the beginning of the paper.

A solution to the problem or answer to the question has been achieved.

Reasons to support the conclusion are stated clearly.

The argument is stated cogently with premises that support the conclusion.

The rules of logic are followed for both deductive and inductive arguments.

The argument avoids fallacies.

The argument shows originality.

Quality of Writing (Chapters 4, 5, 6, 7)

Clarity: The writing is appropriately clear for the audience.

Simplicity: The writing avoids awkwardness and unnecessary complication.

Economy: There is no undue wordiness, padding, repetitiveness, redundancy, misplaced emphasis, or pretentiousness.

Accuracy: The writing conforms to generally accepted rules of grammar and diction.

Style: Paragraphs are appropriate in length and focus.

Style: The writing has pleasing flow.